Christmas

in Texas

Cook Book

edited by

Marie Cahill

GOLDEN WEST ☼ PUBLISHERS

Cover photo by Hal Lott/TexStockPhotoInc.

Acknowledgements

The editor would like to thank all of the Texas cooks and companies who shared their recipes and their Christmas memories; the San Antonio Conservation Society; the Gillespie County Historical Society; Fort Concho National Historic Landmark; and the numerous Chambers of Commerce that provided information. She would also like to express her gratitude to Thora Cahill for her editorial assistance.

Library of Congress Cataloging-in-Publication Data

Cahill, Marie
　　Christmas in Texas Cook Book / by Marie Cahill.
　　　　　p.　　cm.
　　Includes index.
　　1. Christmas cookery　　2. Cookery, International　3. Christmas -
　　- Texas　　I. Title
TX739.2.C45C34　1994　　　　　　　　　　　94-24483
641.5' 68—dc20　　　　　　　　　　　　　　CIP

Printed in the United States of America

ISBN #0-914846-86-8

Second Printing © 1995

Golden West Publishers, Inc.
4113 N. Longview Ave.
Phoenix, AZ 85014, USA
(602) 265-4392

Christmas in Texas

Table of Contents

A Sampling of Christmas Events Across Texas

Amarillo: *Festival in the Park*
Arlington: *Christmas Tree Lighting Ceremony*
Austin: *Totally Texas Christmas*
Beaumont: *Symphony of Trees*
Carmine: *Christmas Arts & Crafts Festival*
Corpus Christi: *Christmas Tree Forest*
Castroville: *Old-Fashioned Christmas*
Conroe: *Christmas in the Pines*
Dallas: *Old City Park Candlelight Tour*
Eustace: *Christmas Parade*
Farmer's Branch: *Christmas Past*
Fort Worth: *Zoobilee of Lights*
Fulton: *A Visit from St. Nicholas*
Galveston: *Dickens on the Strand*
Groesbeck: *Christmas Lighting Contest*
Houston: *Christmas Candlelight Tours*
Jacksboro: *Christmas Tour of Homes*
Jefferson: *Christmas Candlelight Tour*
Laredo: *Christmas Tree Lighting Ceremony*
Lubbock: *Lights on Broadway*
Mineral Wells: *Christmas Tour of Homes*
Montgomery: *Christmas in Old Montgomery*
Mount Vernon: *Colonial Christmas Weekend*
Odessa: *Merry Marketplace*
Port Neches: *Christmas on the Neches Festival*
Richardson: *Christmas Parade*
Round Rock: *Christmas Family Night*
San Angelo: *Christmas at Old Fort Concho*
San Antonio: *Holiday River Festival; Fiestas Navidenas; Christmas Serenade; Las Posadas*
Seabrook/Kemah: *Christmas Boat Parade*
Texarkana: *Christmas Parade; Santa's Secret Village*
Waco: *Christmas on the Brazos*
Wichita Falls: *Fantasy of Lights*

 # Texas at a Glance

Area: Texas is the second largest state in the U. S. (Alaska is first)

Extent: Texas extends about 800 miles north-northwest to south-southeast and about 750 miles east to west.

Population: Texas is now the third largest state in the nation with nearly 18 million persons, preceded only by California and New York.

Capital: Austin

Bird: Mockingbird

Dish: Chili

Fish: Guadalupe Bass

Flower: Bluebonnet

Gem: Texas Blue Topaz

Motto: Friendship

Nickname: Lone Star State

Seal: Five-pointed star enfolded by grain

Shell: Lightning Whelk

Song: *"Texas, Our Texas"*

Stone: Petrified Palmwood

Tree: Pecan

Dickens on the Strand

For one weekend during the Christmas season, Galveston's historic Strand District becomes the site of a Victorian Christmas. The area was built in the 1880s, and though its era as a financial center has long since passed, its iron-front buildings have been preserved, a monument to its former glory days. The heart of the district is The Strand, a street modeled after one of the same name in London. It is this connection to London that inspired *Dickens on the Strand*, a festival of Victorian entertainment and food. The 12-block area becomes host to jugglers, mimes, musicians, carolers and dancers — all in Victorian attire. The food has an equally British flavor, with plum pudding, roasted chestnuts, baked oysters and bangers among the offerings. In conjunction with the event, Dickens' *A Christmas Carol* is performed at the Grand 1894 Opera house.

Christmas at Fort Concho

Every year during the first weekend in December, Old Fort Concho, a national historic landmark, recreates Christmas as it was in the frontier days. Fort Concho was built in 1867 to protect cattle drives and mail routes from the Indians. Over the next 20 years, the fort eventually was home to eight companies, including the 4th Cavalry; the 10th Cavalry, an all-black regiment known as the Buffalo Soldiers; and the headquarters of the US Army's 16th Infantry. By 1889 the need for the fort ended with the close of the Indian Wars. Its presence, however, had paved the way for the town of San Angelo, which grew into a thriving ranching community.

Today, Fort Concho is the nation's largest preserved fort from the Indian War era. Over half of the fort's original buildings have been restored, including a barracks, officers' quarters, hospital and mess hall.

During the holiday season, the fort celebrates its heritage with Christmas at Old Fort Concho. Nine of the officers' quarters are decorated to reflect the fort's history, with each house illustrating a different theme: Victorian, German, Czech, and so on. To add to the authenticity, buildings are lit by candlelight and volunteers dress in period costumes. Festivities include food, dancing, caroling, musical pageants and an arts and crafts fair.

Chapter One

Los Pastores

Christmas in Texas is a multicultural affair. A land of diverse regions, Texas is also a land where many cultures mix. According to one count, 26 different ethnic groups have left their mark on the development of Texas. The Spanish were the first people from another land to arrive in Texas, and their heritage remains the most influential on Texas culture.

The first known Spanish explorer was Alonso Alvarez de Peñeda, who mapped the Texas coast in 1519. About ten years later Alvar Cabeza de Vaca and his companions were shipwrecked along the coast. They spent six years traveling among the Native Americans before returning to Spain with their tales of riches in the New World. Various explorers and Franciscan missionaries arrived over the next 175 years. The French also began to explore the new land, but it was the Spanish who first laid claim to Texas, declaring it a province in 1691.

At Christmas time, Texas comes alive with events that recall its Spanish-Mexican heritage. Perhaps one of the oldest traditions is *Los Pastores* (The Shepherds), a mystery play that has its roots in medieval times. In medieval Spain, the play was used as a teaching tool in an era when few were literate. In the eighteenth century, when Texas was a Spanish province, it provided a way for the Franciscan friars to teach religious doctrine to the native people. Over the centuries, the play was modified by the local Indian and Mexican cultures. Despite the interjection of comic and even illogical characters, the basic theme of the eternal conflict between good and evil has remained. The plot follows the shepherds en route to Bethlehem to visit El Niño Jesus, the Christ Child. As they make their journey, Lucifer and his followers try to stop them. Ultimately, good triumphs over evil when St. Michael strikes down the Devil. The members of the audience then join the performers on stage as they pay homage to the Holy Family.

Performances of *Los Pastores* can be seen throughout all of Texas, but perhaps one of the best known is the annual performance by the San Antonio Conservation Society, which has sponsored a performance of the play at Mission San Jose every year since 1945. This version of *Los Pastores* was found by Don Leandro Granados, who remembered the play from his youth in Mexico. It was written on a used ledger that had been discarded. Don Leandro assembled a group of parishioners at Our Lady of Guadalupe Catholic Church, who performed the play at the church, at the homes of players, and at the homes of residents who valued the play's historical and cultural significance. The pastor of the church, Father Carmelo Tranchese, transcribed and translated the play. The songs that accompany the drama have never been transcribed and are passed down from one generation to the next, just as the play once was.

Don Leandro's version of *Los Pastores* ran about eight hours, but the current version performed by the Guadalupe players has been shortened to approximately two hours. As in times past, the players add, interpret, create and give life to a version that is uniquely their own. The players design and make their own costumes, which are vivid, imaginative and often whimsical. Their shepherds' crooks are adorned with ribbons, bells, and flowers and make delightful music as they are tapped in rhythm to their songs.

Beverages

Holiday Eggnog

"A rich, creamy eggnog that's wonderful for a party."
Imperial Sugar Company, Sugar Land

3 EGG YOLKS
3/4 cup SUGAR
1/4 tsp. SALT
3 cups whole MILK, scalded
1 cup HEAVY CREAM
1 Tbsp. DRY SHERRY
3 EGG WHITES
MULTI-COLORED NONPAREILS

Beat egg yolks thoroughly; mix 1/2 cup sugar and salt and gradually beat into egg yolks. Gradually add scalded milk and cream, beating constantly. Cook in top of double boiler over hot water until mixture is thick enough to coat a spoon. Cool. Add sherry. Chill. When ready to serve, beat egg whites until stiff, gradually beating in remaining sugar; beat until stiff. Fold egg whites into chilled custard. Pour into chilled punch bowl. Sprinkle with nonpareils.

Genuine Texas Margarita

A holiday party would be incomplete without a genuine Texas Margarita. The drink was created somewhere along the Texas-Mexican border. Though numerous restaurants may serve something similar to a frozen slush, there is only one way to drink a Margarita — on the rocks.

1 oz. LIME JUICE
1 oz. TRIPLE SEC
2 oz. TEQUILA

Combine all ingredients. If desired, rub lime juice around rim of glass, flip glass over and dip in saucer of salt. Serve over ice.

Mother's Hot Christmas Punch

"This is a delicious non-alcoholic drink that my mother served to family and friends during the Christmas holidays."
Jody Feldtman Wright, San Antonio

2 qts. PINEAPPLE JUICE
2 qts. APPLE JUICE
1 cup LEMON JUICE
1 lb. BROWN SUGAR
1 cup WHITE SUGAR
2 qts. WATER
12 whole CLOVES
2 CINNAMON STICKS

Place all ingredients in large kettle over open flame. Stir occasionally so sugar will melt. Let mixture boil three minutes. Serve hot.

Christmas Wassail

2 qts. SWEET APPLE CIDER
1 cup LEMON JUICE
2 cups ORANGE JUICE (no pulp)
JUICE from 2 cans (15 1/2 oz. ea.) PINEAPPLE
1 tsp. whole CLOVES
1 CINNAMON STICK
SUGAR to taste

Combine all ingredients and bring to a simmer. Strain and serve hot.

Sugarplum Cranberry Punch

A zesty, festive punch that's fun for a party.

**2 cans (1 lb.) JELLIED
    CRANBERRY SAUCE
3/4 cup BROWN SUGAR
4 cups WATER
3/4 tsp. whole CLOVES
1/2 tsp. CINNAMON
1/4 tsp. NUTMEG
1/2 tsp. ALLSPICE
1/4 tsp. SALT
4 cups unsweetened PINEAPPLE
    JUICE
RED FOOD COLORING
LEMON SLICES**

Crush cranberry sauce with a fork and combine with brown sugar, 1 cup water, spices and salt. Bring to a boil; add pineapple juice and 3 cups water. Heat to boiling and simmer 5 minutes. Color with red food color. Serve in punch bowl or pitcher which has been carefully prewarmed with warm, then hot water. Float lemon slices.

Cranberry Spritzer

**1 bottle (48 oz.) CRANBERRY JUICE COCKTAIL
2 cups PINEAPPLE JUICE**

Combine juices and serve over ice.

Champurro

Champurro is a rich, creamy cocoa drink. It is served hot and can be topped with whipped cream.

1 cup EVAPORATED MILK
1 cup WATER
3 Tbsp. FLOUR
4 Tbsp. COCOA
dash SALT
8 tsp. SUGAR

Heat milk and water to a fast boil, stirring frequently. Reduce heat.

In a mixing bowl, mix flour, cocoa, salt and sugar with 1/4 cup water. Blend until smooth and creamy. Add cocoa mixture to milk mixture and blend in well. Cook over medium heat, stirring constantly until thick. Allow cocoa to come to a carefully-watched bubbly boil. Serve in mugs. Sprinkle with a dash of nutmeg.

Makes 2 cups.

Hot Buttered Wine

1 can (6 oz.) frozen ORANGE JUICE CONCENTRATE
2 cups WATER
2 cups MUSCATEL
1/8 tsp. CINNAMON
1/8 tsp. NUTMEG
1/2 cup SUGAR
1 Tbsp. BUTTER
1/2 fresh LEMON, sliced

Combine all ingredients in a saucepan or chafing dish and stir until sugar dissolves. Heat steaming hot, but do not boil. Serve hot.

Chapter Two

Las Posadas

Las Posadas is another Mexican-Spanish tradition that is looked forward to with anticipation every year at Christmas. *Las Posadas*, which means "the inns", is a recreation of the night of Christ's birth and of Joseph and Mary searching for lodging. The custom was first introduced by Father Diego Soria in the sixteenth century. Originally, the ritual took place over nine days (a novena) from December 16 through the 24th with nine families participating.

Guided by candlelight, one family would go to the home of the other families, seeking lodging as Joseph and Mary had done. Playing the part of Joseph, the head of the family would sing his request, "Mary, my wife, is expecting a child. She must have shelter tonight. Let us in. Let us in." The "innkeeper" would answer in song, "I do not trust you. Go away. Go away."

The next family would follow and so on until eight families had reached the ninth house. This family invited everyone in and the celebrating began. On the ensuing nights the entire ritual would be repeated, each time with a different family playing host.

Today the ritual is generally condensed into one evening. *Las Posadas* is celebrated in numerous neighborhoods throughout Texas, but San Antonio has one of the largest, most festive celebrations on its famous River Walk, or Paseo del Rio, along the San Antonio River. Every December hundreds of participants gather at the River Walk for *Las Posadas*. Guided by candlelight and led by mariachi, the procession makes its way down the River Walk, seeking lodging at various spots. Finally, at the Arneson River Theater the crowd is welcomed by the archbishop and the festivity begins, with cookies and hot chocolate for all.

Oftentimes celebrations of *Las Posadas* end with the breaking of a piñata. Made of clay or papier-mâché in the shape of an animal, a star, or maybe even Santa Claus, the piñata is filled with candy. It is hung above the crowd and all the children (and some of the adults) take a turn trying to break it with a stick while blindfolded. At last someone cracks the shell, and the candy tumbles to the floor amid a mad rush for its delicious hidden treasure.

San Antonio's River Walk is also the site of another Christmas tradition that has gained popularity all over the United States. Every year at Christmas the River Walk is illuminated by thousands of luminarias in *La Fiesta de las Luminarias*, or the *Festival of Lights*. Luminarias were originally small bonfires of piñon boughs but with the addition of a little Yankee ingenuity, they evolved into candles placed in small paper bags weighted with sand. Today, some luminarias are electric lights inside ceramic containers shaped like paper bags. As with *Las Posadas, La Fiesta de las Luminarias* began as a religious ritual commemorating the journey to Bethlehem made by Joseph and Mary, with candles lighting their way.

Meals at Christmas time are filled with Mexican favorites. Chili con carne, posole, turkey with molé sauce and tamales, which may have special fillings of fruit or nuts and seeds. On the sweet side, one can sample buñuelos (fritters covered in cinnamon and sugar), champurro (hot chocolate thickened with corn meal) or leche quemada, a caramel pudding.

Appetizers

Pinwheels

"My most popular appetizer: three ingredients, three steps, three cheers! Pinwheels are a quick and easy appetizer for Christmas or any party. They look like candy when placed side by side on a pretty tray—guests have a pleasant surprise!" Sally Walker, Coldspring

1 pkg. CREAM CHEESE, softened
1 pkg. (16 oz.) sliced DANISH HAM
1 bunch GREEN ONIONS, washed, ends trimmed

Spread cream cheese thinly to entirely coat each ham slice. (Do one at a time). Place one green onion at edge of ham slice (lengthwise) and roll ham over and around onion. Slice "roll" at 1/2 inch intervals. Lay each "Pinwheel" on its side and serve cold. Hint: Wipe knife clean occasionally to keep Pinwheels from looking smeared.

Yield: 7 to 8 dozen.

Hot Spinach Dip

A quick and delicious dip that's great for Christmas parties.

1 lb. VELVEETA® JALAPEÑO CHEESE
1 med. ONION, chopped
1/2 cup MILK
2 oz. PIMENTO, chopped
1 med. TOMATO, chopped
1 pkg. (10 oz.) FROZEN SPINACH, drained

Melt cheese in double boiler or microwave. Add remaining ingredients. Serve warm.

Cheese Ring

"This recipe came from a church friend. She served it at a Christmas party and it was quickly devoured." Beverly McClatchy, Midland

1 lb. SHARP CHEDDAR CHEESE, grated
1 sm. ONION, finely chopped
1 tsp. GARLIC POWDER
3/4 cup MARGARINE
1 tsp. HOT SAUCE
1 cup PECANS, chopped
STRAWBERRY PRESERVES

Mix all ingredients, except strawberry preserves. Shape into a ring and chill. Place preserves in a small bowl in center of ring. Serve with crackers.

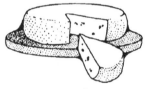

Jalapeño Cheese Bake

Kelly McCulloch, Alvarado

1 lb. CHEDDAR CHEESE, grated
1 lb. MONTEREY JACK CHEESE, grated
1/2 cup JALAPEÑOS, grated
2 EGGS
1 lg. can PET® MILK
1/2 cup FLOUR

Mix two cheeses together. Grease baking dish and place one half of cheese into dish. Add jalapeños and remainder of cheese into dish. Beat eggs and milk together, stir in flour and mix well. Pour over cheese. Bake at 350 degrees for 45 minutes. Cool for 3 hours and cut into squares.

Texas Chili Pecans

"This is something we have before, during and after Christmas because we all love pecans and this recipe has become our favorite way to eat toasted pecans. This recipe has less fat than most toasted pecans and we love all the other ingredients!" Carol Barclay, Portland

4 cups (1 lb.) PECAN HALVES
3 Tbsp. COFFEE-FLAVORED LIQUEUR
1 Tbsp. VEGETABLE OIL
1/4 cup CHILI POWDER
3 Tbsp. SUGAR
1/2 tsp. SALT
1/4 tsp. GROUND RED PEPPER

Preheat oven to 300 degrees. Combine nuts, liqueur and oil in large bowl; toss until well-coated. Add remaining ingredients; toss again. Spread nuts on a jellyroll pan and bake for 25 minutes, stirring frequently. Remove from oven and loosen nuts from pan with metal spatula. Cool in pan on wire rack. Pack in decorative jars or boxes.

Yield: 4 cups.

Pineapple Cheese Balls

2 pkgs. (8 oz. ea.) CREAM CHEESE
1 can (8 1/2 oz.) CRUSHED PINEAPPLE,
    well drained
1/4 cup BELL PEPPER, chopped
2 Tbsp. GREEN ONION, chopped
1 tsp. SALT
2 cups PECANS, chopped

    Soften cream cheese and add remaining ingredients except one cup of the pecans. Shape into balls and roll in remaining pecans.

Zesty Italian Dip

Great colors for a Christmas dip and a wonderful taste!

1 container (8 oz.) SOUR CREAM
1/3 cup RED BELL PEPPER, chopped
1/3 cup GREEN BELL PEPPER, chopped
1 pkg. GOOD SEASONS® ZESTY ITALIAN DRESSING MIX

    Mix all ingredients together and chill.

South Texas Nachos

Two favorites combined into one appetizer!

2 cups WATER
1/2 lb. unpeeled, medium-size FRESH SHRIMP
1 can (4 oz.) DICED GREEN CHILES, drained
1 can (2 1/4 oz.) RIPE OLIVES, pitted, sliced and drained
1 1/2 cups CHEDDAR CHEESE, shredded
1/2 cup MAYONNAISE or SALAD DRESSING
8 dozen ROUND TORTILLA CHIPS

Bring water to a boil; add shrimp, and cook 3 to 5 minutes or until shrimp turns pink. Drain well; rinse with cold water. Peel and devein shrimp; coarsely chop. Combine shrimp, chiles, olives, cheese and mayonnaise. Place tortilla chips on baking sheets; top each with 1 1/2 teaspoons shrimp mixture. Bake at 350 degrees for 5 minutes or until cheese melts.

Yield: 8 dozen.

Festive Mexican Pizza

The bell pepper colors add the festive part!

FLOUR TORTILLAS, any size
SALSA

Toppings:
CHEESE, grated
CHILES, diced
MEAT, cooked and chopped
ONIONS, diced
TOMATOES, sliced or diced
RED and/or GREEN BELL PEPPERS, diced

Spread a thin layer of salsa over flour tortilla. Add toppings. Place on cookie sheet and broil until edges of tortilla turn light brown.

Allow 1 small or one-half large tortilla per serving.

Okra Pinwheels

"My aunt prepares this every holiday for our family gatherings, and when I was asked to bring an appetizer to our company Christmas party, I called my Aunt Tootsie in New Orleans for instructions. This recipe was a big hit, and it is easy and inexpensive." Lynne K. Laque, San Angelo

1 lb. SQUARE HAM SLICES
2 jars (16 oz.) TALK O'TEXAS® CRISP OKRA PICKLES
1 pkg. (8 oz.) CREAM CHEESE, softened
ROUND TOOTHPICKS

First, cut the crown off the okra pods; set aside. Lay a ham slice on flat surface, and spread a generous amount of cream cheese evenly across the ham. Then place okra pods end to end along edge of ham slice and roll evenly. Place three or four toothpicks along seam to hold roll together. Let set overnight, covered, in the refrigerator. When ready to serve, remove toothpicks and slice 1/8 to 1/4 inch thick with a sharp knife. Place on a serving tray. Your guests will love them.

Cheese Meat Ball

This is one of the easiest and best tasting cheese balls you'll ever make. A real party pleaser!

1 pkg. (8 oz.) CREAM CHEESE, softened.
1 pkg. thin sliced BEEF LUNCH MEAT, chopped
1 bunch GREEN ONION, chopped
ACCENT®, to taste

Place cream cheese in a bowl and add lunch meat, onion and Accent. Shape into a ball and serve with crackers.

Summer Sausage

This recipe takes four days to prepare, but is well worth the effort.

2 lb. LEAN GROUND BEEF
1 tsp. LIQUID SMOKE
1/8 tsp. GARLIC POWDER
1/2 tsp. coarse GROUND PEPPER
1/2 tsp. MUSTARD SEED
3 Tbsp. MORTONS® QUICK CURING SALT
1/2 cup WATER

Mix well, cover, and refrigerate.

2nd day: Mix well, cover and refrigerate.

3rd day: Same.

4th day: Mix well, shape in small rolls and bake at 150 degrees for eight hours.

Cheese Straws

1 1/2 cups FLOUR
1/2 cup SHORTENING
1 tsp. BAKING POWDER
1/4 tsp. SALT
4-5 Tbsp. ICE WATER
1 cup CHEDDAR CHEESE, grated
CAYENNE PEPPER, to taste
PAPRIKA

Mix all ingredients except paprika into a dough. Roll thin; cut in narrow strips and place on greased cookie sheet. Bake 12 to 15 minutes at 425 degrees or until lightly browned. Cool. Sprinkle lightly with paprika.

Chapter Three

Christmas in Central Texas

Given the sheer magnitude and geographical diversity of the state, it's not surprising that Texas is divided into regions, or the so-called Five States—North, South, East, West and Central.

The Central region is the hardest to define geographically, as it tends to overlap the other areas, but this area and its people have a strong sense of history. The region still bears the ethnic footprint of the people who first settled here during the influx of European immigration in the mid-1800s and many of their cultural Christmas celebrations are carried on today.

To relive Christmas as it was in the 1800s, a visit to Bastrop is in order. A small town in Central Texas, Bastrop was founded in 1832, which means it was established even before Texas declared itself an independent republic. Bastrop is proud of its heritage and is home to over 130 structures listed in the National Registry of Historic Places, including an Opera House built in 1889. At Christmas, many of the buildings and homes are decorated in holiday splendor. The downtown area is adorned in lights and oftentimes features strolling musicians for the enjoyment of the holiday shoppers. Every year the Crocheran Plantation holds a Christmas celebration with live Christmas cards, a Yule log, and hay rides. Santa Claus also pays a special visit. Bastrop is about 28 miles southeast of Austin.

In New Braunfels, German traditions run strong. The Civic Center hosts a *Weihnachtsmarket*, St. Nicholas Day is celebrated, and German food is highlighted at a candlelight tour of local landmarks. A mingling of Texas-German cultures can be seen in "Cowboy Kringle" at the Market Days Festival. In San Marcos, the banks of its namesake river are transformed into a Christmas wonderland with twinkling lights, music and entertainment. Known as the *Sights and Sounds of Christmas,* this riverside extravaganza has been an annual event since 1986. The event has something for everyone, from Santa's Village, complete with elves scampering about, to *A Night in Old Bethlehem,* a replica of the ancient village. Choirs singing Christmas carols can be heard at the Old Fish Hatchery and children can decorate an old-fashioned Christmas tree at the log schoolhouse.

Round Rock, just north of Austin, kicks off the Christmas holidays with the lighting of its historic downtown area. As in many communities, local productions of the *Messiah* and concerts are highlights of the season.

Austin, the state capital, also lies in Central Texas. The city was originally named Waterloo, but was renamed in honor of Stephen F. Austin, the "Father of Texas", who organized the first American settlement in 1821 when Texas was governed by Mexico. In true Texas style, the state capital boasts the world's largest man-made Christmas tree, illuminated with over 3500 lights. The annual lighting of the tree in Zilker Park is one of the highlights of Austin's Christmas season. The city is also well-known for its Victorian Christmas, a bazaar featuring arts and crafts, period music caroling, Victorian-era street performers, barbershop quartets, choirs and minstrels.

Salads

Vermicelli Salad

Debbie Kremling, Sherman

1 pkg. (12 oz.) VERMICELLI
1 Tbsp. ACCENT®
2 Tbsp. LAWRY'S® SEASONED SALT
3 Tbsp. LEMON JUICE
4 Tbsp. VEGETABLE OIL
1 to 1 1/2 cups MIRACLE WHIP® SALAD DRESSING
1 cup CELERY, chopped
1/2 cup GREEN PEPPER, chopped
1/2 cup ONION, chopped
1/4 cup RIPE OLIVES, chopped
1 jar PIMENTOS

Break vermicelli; cook and rinse. Marinate the vermicelli in Accent, seasoned salt, lemon juice and oil overnight. Add remaining ingredients and toss.

Serves 12 to 14.

Red & Green Jello

1 pkg. LIME JELLO®
1 lb. MARSHMALLOWS
1 pkg. (8 oz.) CREAM CHEESE, softened
1 cup WHIPPED TOPPING
1 cup CRUSHED PINEAPPLE, drained
2 pkg. CHERRY JELLO®

Dissolve lime jello in 2 cups boiling water. Melt marshmallows in jello mix. Cool until slightly thickened. Fold in cream cheese, whipped topping and crushed pineapple. Place mixture in large oblong pan. Dissolve cherry jello in 4 cups boiling water. Cool and add to top of lime jello.

Toasted Texas Pecan Salad
with Dallas Goat Cheese & Apples

Paula S. Lambert, The Mozzarella Company, Dallas

1/2 cup toasted TEXAS PECANS, coarsely chopped
1 GREEN APPLE, peeled and thinly sliced
1 tsp. LEMON JUICE
1/2 head ROMAINE LETTUCE
1/2 head RED LETTUCE
4 oz. DALLAS GOAT CHEESE, crumbled

Toast pecans, slice apples and toss with lemon juice. Tear lettuce into pieces. Place all ingredients in salad bowl and toss gently with dressing.

Dressing:
1/3 cup EXTRA VIRGIN OLIVE OIL
1 Tbsp. BALSAMIC VINEGAR
1 Tsp. LEMON JUICE
1/2 tsp. SALT
FRESHLY GROUND PEPPER

Whisk together all ingredients.
Serves 4.

Cranberry Freeze Salad

1 can WHOLE CRANBERRIES
1 can (8 oz.) CRUSHED PINEAPPLE, drained
1 cup SOUR CREAM

Mix and freeze in 8-inch square pan. Cut into squares before serving.

Vegetable Salad

"This recipe is for the health-oriented folks. It is red, green and white—looks lovely when served in a crystal bowl. I never fail to get requests for the recipe when I take it to a large gathering. It is especially wonderful during the busy holidays, not only for its festive colors, but because it is prepared up to 24 hours before serving time." Pauline Huneycutt, San Antonio

1 lg. bunch BROCCOLI, cut to bite-size pieces
1 lg. head CAULIFLOWER, cut to bite-size pieces
1 lg. bunch RADISHES, sliced
1 bunch GREEN ONIONS, sliced
6 slices BACON, fried crisp, drained and torn
    into bite-size pieces

Toss all ingredients together in a large bowl and add dressing. Refrigerate overnight before serving.

Dressing:

2 Tbsp. SUGAR
2 Tbsp. APPLE CIDER VINEGAR
1/2 cup low-fat MIRACLE WHIP® SALAD DRESSING
1/2 cup low-fat RANCH DRESSING
SALT and PEPPER to taste

Combine all ingredients in a shaker. Pour over salad. Serves 12.

Hawaiian Sweet Potato Salad

"Since one can make an Irish Potato Salad, I did not see why a salad could not be made with sweet potatoes. As sweet potatoes are often associated with holiday dinners, adding the red and green cherries makes a festive, tasty dish." Jean Fourmentin, Wellington

2 med. SWEET POTATOES, cooked, cooled and cubed
1 sm. can PINEAPPLE TIDBITS
1/2 cup COCONUT
1 cup PECANS, chopped
1 cup colored MINIATURE MARSHMALLOWS
1 small jar red and/or green MARASCHINO CHERRIES
1/2 cup MAYONNAISE

Combine above ingredients except mayonnaise, reserving the juice from the pineapple to make the dressing. Take 1/2 cup mayonnaise to which the juice has been added a little at a time until the right consistency has been reached. Pour over potato mixture. Mix and let set in refrigerator about 2 hours for ingredients to blend. The cherries may be mixed in or put on top as a garnish. Put the salad in a pretty clear glass dish or casserole.

Cranberry Medley Salad

A fresh, tart and sweet salad.

1 lb. fresh CRANBERRIES
1 lb. GREEN SEEDLESS GRAPES
1 cup MINIATURE MARSHMALLOWS
1 cup NUTS, chopped
1 cup HEAVY CREAM, whipped
1/4 cup BROWN SUGAR, packed

Grind cranberries in food chopper or blender. Combine with remaining ingredients. Chill. Serve on lettuce leaves on salad plates.

Grapefruit Salad

"We lived in the Rio Grande Valley, and the harvest of the grapefruit is at its height around Christmas, so this salad was always a favorite — as it is now!" Jody Feldtman Wright, San Antonio

2 pkg. KNOX® GELATIN
1/4 cup cold WATER
1/2 cup boiling WATER
3 Tbsp. LEMON JUICE
1 cup SUGAR
3 cups GRAPEFRUIT SECTIONS
1/4 cup NUTS, chopped

In a 1 1/2-quart bowl, sprinkle gelatin in cold water; let stand 1 minute. Add boiling water. Add lemon juice and sugar and stir until dissolved. Add grapefruit sections and nuts. Refrigerate.

Serves 8.

Elly's Cole Slaw

This dish is served at the Guadalupe Smoked Meat Company Restaurant in New Braunfels.

1 head CABBAGE, finely chopped
1/2 cup canned SWEET RED PEPPERS, rinsed well
1/2 cup GREEN OLIVES, chopped
1/2 cup SOUR CREAM
1 cup MAYONNAISE
1/2 Tbsp. GARLIC SALT
1/2 tsp. BLACK PEPPER

Combine the first three ingredients. In a separate bowl, mix sour cream, mayonnaise, garlic salt and pepper. Add to the first three ingredients.

Plum Salad

"This dish is great with turkey, game, brisket...just about anything. It had become a holiday favorite with my family. An old woman back in my home town gave me this recipe so long ago that her instructions were 'to push the plums through a sieve' and 'mash the cream cheese with a fork.' I adapted the recipe to the blender many years ago." Faye Albertson, Wimberley

3 Tbsp. SALAD DRESSING
1 sm. pkg. LEMON JELLO®
1 can RED, GREEN OR PURPLE PLUMS (drain and save juice)
1 pkg. KNOX® GELATIN
1 cup HOT WATER
1 lg. pkg. CREAM CHEESE, softened
1/2 cup PECANS, chopped

Grease a 9-inch square glass dish (or mold) with 1 tablespoon of the salad dressing. Dissolve the lemon jello in 1 cup of hot water and 1 cup of the plum juice. Dissolve gelatin in the rest of plum juice and add to hot jello mixture. Remove seeds from plums. Discard seeds and place plums in blender. Cube the cream cheese and place in blender. Add the remaining two tablespoons of salad dressing and the jello mixture to the blender. Blend just a few seconds. Pour into greased dish and top with chopped pecans. Chill until set and cut into squares for serving.

Pineapple Cheese Salad

"This recipe comes from my Aunt Ruth Dodson. My family has used this recipe for Christmas since the 1950s. It is a wonderful salad." Mary Foster, Wellington.

1 sm. can CRUSHED PINEAPPLE
2/3 cup SUGAR
1 pkg. GELATIN
1 cup COLD WATER
1/2 pint WHIPPING CREAM
1 cup PECANS, chopped
1 cup SHARP CHEESE, grated

Heat pineapple and sugar; soften gelatin in cold water and add to pineapple and bring to boil. Chill until partly set. Whip cream and fold in with nuts and cheese. Chopped pimento can be added, if desired.

Pink Salad

"I have made this salad for years for our family parties."
Sylvia Meador, Boyd

1 can SWEETENED CONDENSED MILK
1 can CHERRY PIE FILLING
1/4 cup LEMON JUICE
1 container (8 oz.) WHIPPED TOPPING
1 sm. can CRUSHED PINEAPPLE
1/4 tsp. ALMOND EXTRACT
1 cup PECANS, chopped
Several drops RED FOOD COLORING

Mix ingredients in order listed and chill well.
Serves 12.

Chinese Chicken Salad

An ideal entree for a Christmas luncheon.

6 Tbsp. SEASONED RICE VINEGAR
2 tsp. SUGAR
2 tsp. SESAME OIL
1 Tbsp. SOY SAUCE
2 1/2 cups COOKED CHICKEN, shredded
4 cups ICEBERG LETTUCE, shredded
4 cups PURPLE CABBAGE, shredded
1 cup ROMA TOMATOES, halved
1/2 cup GREEN ONION, coarsely chopped
1/2 cup fresh CILANTRO LEAVES
ORIENTAL NOODLES

In a large bowl combine vinegar, sugar, oil, soy sauce and chicken. Add lettuce, cabbage, tomatoes, onions and cilantro; mix. Add additional soy sauce to taste. Prepare noodles according to package directions. Serve salad on bed of noodles.

Serves 4 to 6.

Orange Gelatin Salad

A popular salad with children at holiday time.

1 can MANDARIN ORANGES
1 pkg. (3 oz.) ORANGE JELLO®
1 container (8 oz.) WHIPPED TOPPING
1 cup COTTAGE CHEESE

Drain oranges. Take juice and enough water to make 1 cup and bring to a boil with the jello. Cool. Chop oranges and mix with whipped topping. Add cottage cheese and mix well. Blend with cooled jello and refrigerate until set.

Serves 10 to 12.

Chapter Four

A Texas-German Christmas

Shortly after Texas joined the United States in 1845, many European immigrants made their way across the ocean in search of a better life. Among the many people who made their new homes in Texas were the Germans. To this day there is still a sizable German population in central Texas.

The first permanent German settlement was in Industry, which took its name from the cigar factory that was the town's major industry. A number of the early German settlers gravitated to the port cities of Galveston and Indianola. From the coast, many journeyed by oxcart or on foot to San Antonio and the surrounding area. San Antonio eventually became the center of German influence in the state and today many of the fine homes built by the German immigrants along the San Antonio River serve as a reminder of the city's German heritage.

In 1848, Ed Steves, a cabinetmaker, was one of the first Germans to arrive in San Antonio. He opened a mill and a mill-working yard, becoming one of the area's most prosperous businessmen. He built a Victorian mansion on King William Street and outfitted it with a formal garden, a fountain purchased at the Philadelphia Centennial Exposition, and an indoor swimming pool. Today, the Steves mansion is part of the San Antonio Conservation Society. It is open to the public and during the Christmas season is decorated in a style that reflects its German Victorian heritage.

Founded in 1846, Fredericksburg was one of the first

German settlements and is still heavily German today. A look at the town's past can be experienced every Christmas during the Candlelight Tour of Homes, sponsored by members of the Gillespie County Historical Society.

One of the best-loved symbols of Christmas, the Christmas tree, can trace its origin to Germany. Christmas trees were a rarity when the first German settlers arrived in the United States. The more staid citizens of eastern communities, such as Boston or Philadelphia, frowned upon the trees because of their roots in pagan traditions, but the more open-minded Texans embraced the custom. In Germany, the trees were usually fir, but in Texas, the settlers were forced to turn to native varieties of evergreens such as juniper and cedar. Typical decorations included popcorn chains, flowers and chains made out of paper, cookies, candy and nuts wrapped in brightly colored paper, fresh fruit and, of course, lots of candles. In many German families, the adults decorated the tree behind closed doors on Christmas Eve. Then, after Christmas Eve services, the children rushed into the room to find their presents waiting from them under a beautiful tree awash in candlelight.

After celebrating Christmas Eve and Christmas Day with family members, the German settlers celebrated Second Christmas, or Zweite Weihnacten, on December 26. This was a day set aside for visiting friends in town or on other ranches. Merrymaking ranged from dances, such as polkas and waltzes, to games like dominoes and pinochle. The German influence also left its mark on Texas cooking. One theory holds that the German custom of roasting a calf, sheep or pig on market day played a part in the development of the famous Texas barbecue. Another Texas tradition—chicken-fried steak—may owe something to German schnitzel. Proponents of this theory point out the similarities between the two dishes, as both are breaded and pan-fried cuts of meat. Of course, German culinary traditions are quite evident during the Christmas season. Many a Texas-German cook is noted for her baking expertise.

Main Dishes

Roast Turkey

Many of the early Texas settlers had been accustomed to roast goose for Christmas dinner. Since geese were hard to come by in their new homeland, they turned to the more readily available wild turkeys. The head of the household would get his shotgun and go find a big bird or two for the family get-together. Nowadays, Texans still enjoy a succulent roast turkey for Christmas, but most folks procure one from their local supermarket.

1 TURKEY
BUTTER or MARGARINE
SALT
PEPPER

Remove giblets and reserve for gravy. Rinse turkey with cold water. Stuff the body and neck cavities before trussing. *Rub butter or margarine all over turkey. Sprinkle with salt and pepper. Place breast side down on rack in roasting pan. Roast in 325 degree oven, allowing 12 minutes per pound. Baste with melted butter every 20 to 30 minutes. Turn turkey over after 1 1/2 hours. Turkey is done when meat thermometer registers 180 degrees in breast meat, 185 degrees in thigh meat. Remove to platter and make gravy.

*See the chapter on side dishes for a tasty selection of recipes for dressings to complement your roast turkey.

Black-Eyed Texas Casserole

"This is a good dish for Christmas Eve dinner or New Year's. The black-eyed pea is a good, versatile vegetable. I survived on them during the Great Depression and still enjoy a steaming bowl cooked with salt pork and served with cornbread and a slice of onion." Lena Vaughan, Wellington

1 1/2 lbs. GROUND ROUND
1 lg. ONION, chopped
2 cloves GARLIC, minced
1 can (15 oz.) BLACK-EYED PEAS
  with JALAPEÑOS, drained
1 can (14 oz.) ENCHILADA SAUCE
1 can CREAM OF CHICKEN SOUP
1 can CREAM OF MUSHROOM SOUP
1 can (10 oz.) TOMATOES with GREEN CHILES, chopped
12-14 CORN TORTILLAS, cut in eighths
2 cups CHEDDAR CHEESE, grated

In a skillet, cook ground round, onion and garlic until browned. Drain. Add black-eyed peas, enchilada sauce, both soups and tomatoes. Layer meat mixture and tortillas in a greased casserole dish. Top with grated cheese. Bake in a pre-heated 350 degree oven for 30 minutes or until bubbly.

Barbecued Chicken

2 CHICKENS (2 to 2 1/2 lbs. ea.)
1/4 lb. BUTTER
4 Tbsp. HEINZ 57® SAUCE
2 Tbsp. prepared MUSTARD
1/2 cup LEMON JUICE
4 Tbsp. TARRAGON
  VINEGAR
1 Tbsp. ground RED CHILE

Split chickens in half lengthwise and break joints of hips, wings and drumsticks so they will stay flat during cooking. Wash and pat dry.

Melt butter and mix with rest of ingredients. Put chicken on an open grill and brush frequently with sauce. Cook until done through (about 45 minutes).

Chicken Tetrazzini

An excellent dish for a family gathering.

1 pkg. (10 oz.) MACARONI or SPAGHETTI
1 lg. can MUSHROOMS, sliced
1 GREEN PEPPER, chopped
1 md. jar PIMENTOS, chopped
WHITE SAUCE
3 cups cooked CHICKEN, chopped

Cook pasta in water or chicken broth. Drain and mix with mushrooms, green pepper and pimentos. Set aside and make white sauce. Add chicken and pasta combination to white sauce. Pour into large oven-proof baking dish and bake at 375 degrees for 30 minutes.

Serves 18.

White Sauce:

2 sticks BUTTER or MARGARINE
2/3 cup FLOUR
1 qt. MILK
SALT and PEPPER to taste
1 lb. CHEDDAR CHEESE, grated

Melt the butter in a heavy skillet. Add flour, stirring constantly about two minutes. Don't let the sauce brown. Add the milk, continuing to stir as the sauce thickens. Bring sauce to a boil. Season with salt and pepper. Lower heat, add cheese and continue to cook for 2 to 3 minutes, stirring constantly.

Shrimp Gumbo

"This is a superb Cajun recipe for Christmas, New Year's and all year long." Glenn Koteras, Orchard

6 tbsp. VEGETABLE OIL	1 lb. OKRA, cut into
3 Tbsp. FLOUR	1/4-inch rounds
1 lg. ONION, chopped	1/2 cup GREEN BELL
2 cloves GARLIC, chopped	PEPPER, chopped
1 sm. can ROTEL® TOMATOES	1 tsp. GUMBO FILÉ
1/2 cup CELERY, chopped	3 tsp. SALT
8 cups WATER	1/2 tsp. PEPPER
2 lb. SHRIMP, peeled	Touch BEER (optional)

In an 8-quart pot, bring oil to smoking point; add flour and stir over low heat until deep brown to make a roux. Add onion and garlic to roux and simmer until onion is clear. Add tomatoes. Cook slowly 15 minutes, add celery and cook another five minutes. Add water and boil briskly about 40 minutes, or until desired consistency. Add shrimp and cook slowly 30 minutes. Add okra and cook 10 minutes or until tender. Add bell pepper, filé, salt and pepper. Add beer if desired. Stir, cover pot and let stand a few minutes. Serve over steamed rice.

Serves 8 - 10.

Chicken Fried Steak

Paul Joenk, Houston

1 lb. ROUND STEAK, cut	1 EGG, beaten
into 4 sections	2 Tbsp. WATER
SEASONED FLOUR*	1/2 cup OIL

*Combine 1/2 cup flour, 1/2 tsp. salt, 1/2 tsp. paprika, 1/2 tsp. pepper. Beat egg, add water and mix well. Dredge steak pieces in flour mixture, dip in egg mixture, and dredge again in flour mixture. Brown on both sides in hot oil in skillet. Cover and cook slowly 20-30 minutes.

Crayfish & Sauce

4 Tbsp. VEGETABLE OIL
1 Tbsp. FLOUR
1 lg. ONION, chopped
3 cloves GARLIC, chopped
1 can (8 oz.) TOMATO SAUCE
1 Tbsp. SUGAR
3 cups WATER
1 1/2 lb. CRAYFISH

In a 4-quart pot, brown flour in oil until deep brown. Add onion, garlic and tomato sauce and simmer for about five minutes. Add sugar and water and bring to a boil. Boil mixture until it reaches desired consistency and add crayfish. Simmer for about 30 minutes. Serve with side dish of rice.

Serves 6.

Holiday Mexican Steaks

"This recipe is wonderful served with picante sauce and hot flour tortillas. I serve this recipe on Christmas morning, but it is good all year round too." Carmen Dougherty, Marion

3 Tbsp. SHORTENING
2 BEEF ROUND STEAKS, trimmed and diced into cubes
SALT and PEPPER to taste
1/2 tsp. GARLIC SALT
2 sm. ONIONS, chopped
1 can (8 oz.) WHOLE TOMATOES, chopped
1 can (4 oz.) GREEN CHILES, chopped
WATER to cover mixture

In large skillet, melt shortening and brown cubed meat with salt, pepper and garlic salt. When meat is browned, add remaining ingredients. Simmer for 30 to 35 minutes, until meat is done and mixture is not too soupy.

Pasta Caprese
with Roasted Peppers, Dallas Goat Cheese & Garlic

6 roasted BELL PEPPERS, cut into strips
1 clove GARLIC, minced
1/4 cup OLIVE OIL
1 lb. PASTA
1/2 lb. fresh DALLAS GOAT CHEESE
Fresh BASIL LEAVES
SALT and PEPPER to taste

Roast bell peppers on grill or under broiler turning until completely blackened. Place in bowl and cover with plastic wrap for 15 to 30 minutes. Remove blackened skin and seeds, and then cut peppers into strips. Sprinkle garlic over peppers and drizzle with olive oil. Set peppers aside to marinate. This can be done several days ahead of time, or just before serving. Cook pasta in rapidly boiling water. When pasta is cooked al dente, drain and place in serving bowl. Crumble goat cheese over pasta and sprinkle thinly cut strips of basil leaves on top, reserving some leaves to use as a garnish. Season with salt and pepper to taste. Toss pasta well. Pour peppers and olive oil over pasta. Toss once more lightly. Garnish with fresh basil leaves.

Serves 4 - 6.

Christmas Ham

1/2 HAM, shank end   **1/2 cup WATER**
3/4 cup ORANGE JUICE   **2 tsp. DRY MUSTARD**
1/2 cup BROWN SUGAR

Score the outside of the ham in a diamond pattern. Place a whole clove in the center of each diamond. Combine orange juice, brown sugar, water and dry mustard. Bake in 325 degree oven for about two hours, basting several times. Ham is done when meat thermometer registers 160 degrees.

Pasta Siciliana
with Red Peppers, Garlic & Fresh Dallas Mozzarella

2 cloves GARLIC
3 RED BELL PEPPERS, cut into strips
OLIVE OIL
1 lb. PASTA
SALT and PEPPER to taste
DRIED OREGANO to taste
1/2 lb. fresh MOZZARELLA, shredded

Sauté garlic and bell pepper strips in olive oil until soft. Cook pasta in rapidly boiling water. When pasta is cooked al dente, drain and place in serving bowl. Pour peppers and olive oil over pasta. Season with salt, pepper and oregano to taste. Toss well. Add mozzarella and toss briefly to distribute mozzarella throughout. The hot pasta melts the mozzarella in a minute or two.

Serves 4 - 6.

Five Cheese Pasta

1 lb. fresh PASTA, such as fettucine
1/4 lb. MASCARPONE
1/4 lb. fresh HERBED GOAT CHEESE, crumbled
1/4 lb. TEXAS BASIL CACIOTTA, shredded
1/4 lb. fresh FETA, coarsely chopped
1/4 lb. goat's milk MONTASIO, grated
Fresh BASIL LEAVES

Cook the pasta in rapidly boiling water for a few minutes until cooked al dente. Drain the pasta in a colander and place in a casserole. Add the mascarpone and goat cheese to the pasta and toss well. Next add the caciotta, feta and half the montasio and toss well. Season with salt and pepper to taste. Sprinkle the remaining montasio on top. Place the casserole under the broiler for a minute or two so that the top is golden brown. Garnish with fresh basil. Serve immediately.

Festive Chicken & Spaghetti Casserole

"I made this dish up years ago. The red pimentos, green peppers and white spaghetti give it a festive look. I always make this casserole to go with our family Christmas dinner, and everyone raves about it. My husband has a Christmas party at work where the wives send the food, so I started sending this casserole. Now they won't let me stop sending it. You can also make this dish after Christmas with leftover turkey and canned broth." Nancy Rhodes, Tenaha

1 1/2 qts. WATER
4 CHICKEN BREASTS, boneless and skinless
2 tsp. POULTRY SEASONING
1 tsp. SALT
1/4 tsp. BLACK PEPPER
CHICKEN BROTH (reserve from chicken)
1 Tbsp. VEGETABLE OIL
1 BELL PEPPER
1/2 bunch GREEN ONIONS, chopped
1/2 stalk CELERY, finely chopped
1 clove GARLIC, minced
1 can CREAM OF MUSHROOM SOUP
1 1/2 Tbsp. SOY SAUCE
1 jar PIMENTOS
1 pkg (10 oz.) SPAGHETTI
1/2 cup SOUR CREAM
5 oz. CHEDDAR CHEESE, grated

Place the water in a stew pot, and boil the chicken, poultry seasoning, salt and pepper until tender. Remove chicken and chop into bite size pieces. Reserve the broth. Heat the vegetable oil in a skillet over high heat, lower to medium heat, and cook bell pepper, green onions, celery and garlic for three minutes. Add mushroom soup, 1 cup of the reserved chicken broth, soy sauce and pimentos. Set

(Continued next page)

aside. Add enough water to 1 cup of the reserved broth to cook the spaghetti according to directions. When spaghetti is done, add sour cream and place in a 8 1/2 x 9 1/2 x 3 casserole. Add chopped chicken and vegetables. Pour 1 cup chicken broth over all. Bake at 350 degrees for 25 minutes. Remove from oven and add cheese to top. Bake for an additional 10 minutes.

Recipe can be made up to three days in advance and reheated when ready to eat.

Green Enchiladas

1 sm. ONION
2 to 3 Tbsp. MARGARINE
1 can CREAM OF CHICKEN SOUP
1 sm. can EVAPORATED MILK
1/2 lb. SOFT PROCESSED CHEESE
1 sm. can GREEN CHILES, chopped
1 sm. can PIMENTOS
1/2 lb. LONGHORN CHEESE, grated
12 CORN TORTILLAS

Sauté onion in margarine until clear. Meanwhile, heat soup, milk and processed cheese in top of double boiler or in microwave until cheese is melted. Add chiles and pimentos. Combine longhorn cheese with onion. Fill each tortilla with cheese and onion mixture. Roll tightly and place in 13 x 9 baking dish. Pour cheese sauce over tortillas. Cover with foil. Bake at 350 degrees for 30 minutes.

Christmas Eve Pizza Casserole

"Every Christmas Eve we all gather at our daughter's house and everyone takes something for dinner. It has become one of our traditions to have this pizza casserole. We all love pizza, so this is perfect." Carol Barclay, Portland

4 oz. uncooked SPAGHETTI
1/4 lb. sliced PEPPERONI
1/2 lb. GROUND BEEF, browned
1 med. ONION, chopped
4 Tbsp. BUTTER, melted and divided
1 GREEN PEPPER, chopped
16 oz. TOMATO SAUCE, divided
1 cup grated SWISS CHEESE, divided
16 oz. sliced MOZZARELLA CHEESE, divided
4 oz. canned chopped MUSHROOMS, drained
1/2 tsp. OREGANO
1/2 tsp. BASIL

Cook spaghetti according to package directions. Boil pepperoni in water for 5 minutes to remove fat; drain. In medium skillet, sauté onion in one tablespoon butter until soft. Remove from skillet and sauté bell pepper in 1 tablespoon butter until partially soft. Preheat oven to 350 degrees. Pour remaining butter into 9 x 13 baking dish. Toss spaghetti in butter. Cover with 8 ounces tomato sauce. In order, add half of Swiss cheese, pepperoni, half of mozzarella, all mushrooms and onions. Next spread browned ground beef, oregano, basil and green peppers. Top with remainder of Swiss cheese, sauce and mozzarella. Bake 20 to 25 minutes.

Serves 10 to 12.

MERRY CHRISTMAS

Sour Cream Chicken Enchiladas

El Galindo Mexican Foods, Austin

4 CHICKEN BREAST HALVES, skinned and boned
4 Tbsp. MARGARINE
1 1/2 cups SOUR CREAM
1 can (10 3/4 oz.) CREAM OF MUSHROOM SOUP
1/2 can (10 oz.) diced TOMATO and GREEN
    CHILES with juice
1 cup MONTEREY JACK CHEESE, shredded
1 med. ONION, grated
10 FLOUR TORTILLAS

Preheat oven to 350 degrees. Simmer chicken breasts in lightly salted water until tender, about 20 minutes, and shred. Set aside. In a large skillet melt margarine. Stir in sour cream, mushroom soup, and tomatoes and green chiles. Set aside 1/2 cup of the cheese and 1 cup of the sour cream mixture. Dip each tortilla in the sour cream mixture; fill with 1/10 of the chicken, cheese and onion. Roll and place in a 13 x 9 baking pan. Repeat with remaining 9 tortillas. Top with cheese and sour cream mixture. Bake covered for 45 minutes. Uncover and brown slightly until bubbly.

Serves 5.

Note: Serve with a green salad with avocado dressing. This dish may be frozen for up to one month. If refrigerated or frozen, allow extra baking time.

Green Corn Tamales

12 ears tender WHITE CORN (save husks)
1 cup MILK
1 1/2 Tbsp. SALT
1 cup SHORTENING
1/2 cup MARGARINE (or butter)
2 cups grated LONGHORN CHEESE
12 ANAHEIM CHILES, fresh or canned

Cut the ends of the corn with a sharp knife, then remove husks. Save all husks. Remove corn silk and wash corn. Remove corn from cobs and grind as finely as possible in food processor or blender. Place in mixing bowl. Add milk, salt, shortening, margarine or butter and mix. Put mixture in blender and blend at high speed, adding small amounts of milk if corn becomes dry.

When corn mixture is well mixed, place in large mixing bowl once again. Blend in cheese with a large mixing spoon. Corn mixture should have a smooth and spreadable texture. This will be the "masa" although it will be fluffier and more moist than regular masa.

Roast green chiles in oven at 350 degrees until fully roasted. Remove skins and seeds, wash, and cut into long strips.

Choose larger husks and rinse in cold water and drain. Using a tablespoon, spoon corn mixture (masa) on wider end of corn husks. Spread evenly but not thickly to cover most of the corn husk but not the narrow end or tail of the husk. Add strips of chiles and if desired, sprinkle 1 tablespoon grated longhorn cheese over chiles. Roll husk to cover masa and chiles and tuck husk tail up. Set upright so that masa shows. Repeat until the masa is all used.

Cook tamales in a steamer or large cooking pot. If you use a cooking pot, line with aluminum foil or extra corn

(Continued next page)

husks. Place tamales in upright position with a crumpled ball of foil at the center to help hold tamales in place. Continue adding tamales in an overlapping fashion so that they hold each other up. Add 1 cup of water carefully to side of pot. Try not to get tamales wet. Let boil, covered, then cook over medium heat for 45 minutes to an hour. Check tamales every 20 minutes and add approximately 1/2 cup water to keep tamales from becoming too dry. Tamales are ready when they are easily removed from the husk. Total preparation time: 2 1/2 hours.

Makes 30 tamales.

Cowgirl Lasagna

1 stick MARGARINE
1 ONION, chopped
1 can GREEN CHILES
1 can CREAM OF CHICKEN SOUP
1 can CREAM OF MUSHROOM SOUP
1 BEEF BOUILLON CUBE
1 can CHICKEN STOCK
1 bag (10 oz.) TORTILLA CHIPS
1 FRYER, boiled, boned, and cut into bite-size pieces
1 pkg. (10 oz) SHARP CHEDDAR CHEESE, grated
1 pkg. (10 oz.) MONTEREY JACK CHEESE, grated

In large skillet, melt margarine, add onion and green chiles and simmer for 10 minutes. Add cans of soup, bouillon, and chicken stock and boil for 1 minute; then simmer 10 minutes. In a 9 x 13 baking dish, place layers of chips, chicken and cheeses, ending with cheese on top. Bake at 350 degrees for 45 minutes.

Chicken Molé

6 whole **CHICKEN BREASTS**
8 to 10 dried **CHILES**, combinations, mostly mild
6 Tbsp. **VEGETABLE OIL**
3/4 cup **WATER**
2 Tbsp. chopped **ONION**
1 diced **GARLIC CLOVE**
1 medium **TOMATO**, chopped
2 toasted **BREAD SLICES**, cubed
2 Tbsp. **RAISINS** (or dates)
2 Tbsp. **PEANUTS**
1/2 tsp. **CINNAMON**, ground
1/4 tsp. **CLOVES**, ground
3 to 4 cups **CHICKEN BROTH**,
    (reserved from stock)
2 Tbsp. **COCOA**
2 tsp. **SUGAR**
SALT to taste

Remove skin from chicken breasts and rinse chicken. Place in large pot and cover with water. Cover and cook until tender. Remove stock and strain. Reserve stock and set chicken aside.

Remove stems from dried chiles and break into small pieces. Fry in 3 tablespoons oil for a few minutes. Drain. Put chiles in blender with approximately 3/4 cup water and purée. Pass through a sieve for a smooth paste. Set aside.

In a saucepan, heat 1 tablespoon oil and sauté bread cubes. In a blender, purée onion, garlic, tomato, sautéed bread cubes, raisins, peanuts, cinnamon and cloves. Heat 2 tablespoons oil and cook mixture over medium heat for 8 minutes. Add chili purée and cook 5 minutes. Blend in 3 to 4 cups chicken broth. Add cocoa, sugar and salt. Cover and simmer 1 1/2 hours, stirring occasionally. Cook uncovered until thick.

Preheat oven to 350 degrees. Place chicken breasts in lightly buttered casserole and pour molé over all. Bake for 10 to 15 minutes, long enough for chicken to be fully heated. Serves 6.

The World Championship Chili Cook-off

The art of fixing chili has been a time-honored Texas tradition since the mid-1800s. Today the official state dish of Texas, chili was developed along the cattle trails of old when chuckwagon cooks, inspired by the area's Mexican cooking traditions, combined their limited supplies with a little ingenuity. There are probably as many recipes for chili as there are Texans, and most Texans are more than willing to discuss the merits of their particular "bowl of red." In fact, the state hosts a number of chili cook-offs, the first and probably most famous being the annual World Championship Chili Cook-off in Terlingua. The Terlingua cook-off was inaugurated when Allen Smith, a New York journalist, boasted he could make a better bowl of chili than any Texan. Those were fighting words to Frank X. Tolbert, food columnist for the Dallas Morning News, who organized a cook-off between Smith and Wick Fowler, a Texas cook. The event was staged at high noon in the abandoned mining town of Terlingua in October 1967. The judges were unable to declare a winner, claiming their taste buds were paralyzed by the chili. Despite the inconclusive results, the event became an annual affair. Held the first weekend in November, the cook-off is so popular that the town's population of 25 swells to over 7000 for the festivities.

*Here's a chili recipe from Jardine's Texas Foods using **D. L. Jardine's Original Texas Chili Kit**®. As Ashley Jardine explains, "as Texans it would be very difficult to imagine the holidays without a hot bowl of authentic chili."*

Jardine's Texas Foods, Buda

Dan Jardine's Original Ranch House Chili

1. After adding **a tablespoon of oil** to your fryin' pan (keeps the meat from stickin') sear **2 pounds of meat** until all redness has turned gray. Use diced meat (about the size of your thumbnail — unless you're a Texan, then only half the size) of coarse ground meat. Don't waste your money on expensive cuts of meat. Use chuck, round, stew meat, pork shoulder, bacon, venison, sausage links, armadillo, yard birds (chicken), or a combination of your own choosing. Our favorite is a real meaty chili with **1 lb. of diced or coarse ground chuck beef** and **1 lb. of a combination of ground and diced pork.** Drain off excess fat from cooked meat and set aside.

2. Now, in a chili kettle (5 qt. or larger Dutch oven) put about **2 Tbsp. of oil.** At medium to high heat stir and add **1 medium onion** and **4 tomatillos, diced.** Heat and stir until onions become transparent.

3. Add the drained meat to the chili kettle and mix well.

4. While stirrin' add **3 1/2 cups fresh spring water** (tap water acceptable), **4 oz. beer** (If you don't condone beer leave it out and try to enjoy your chili anyhow), **1 can (8 oz.) tomato sauce, 1 can (14 1/2 oz.) store bought tomatoes (including juice), 1 can (6 oz.) tomato paste** and dump in the contents of the **two large paks** of our **Texas Chili spice blend** and the **paks of celery and bell pepper.** Use the **salt paks and salt to taste.** Mix well

and turn down to simmer.

5. Now it's time to add a little caliente bite to the chili. The amount of caliente (hot) **crushed red peppers** that you choose to add to the chili kettle will determine the chili's degree of authenticity and warmth. If you're feeding little kids, grandmothers, or east-coast sissies, it's best to forget the pak of crushed red caliente peppers. For chili that's hot enough to barely make your forehead sweat, add up to 1/2 teaspoon of the enclosed pak of crushed red peppers. Dump in up to 2 teaspoons of hot red peppers for a Texas chili that's hotter'n a two dollar pistol on Saturday night and a guaranteed sure-fire remedy for sinus problems or whatever else ails you. We suggest that you change spoons often while stirrin'. This will prevent the spoon's meltin' or catchin' on fire from chili heat. Return lid to kettle and let simmer for 45 minutes. Add fresh spring water as needed to keep the whole mess from burnin'. Salt to taste.

6. About 30 minutes before you're ready to dig in, it's time to add **one or two cans (15 oz. ea.) of pinto beans (kidney beans will do).** If you're one of those that don't appreciate frijoles, then leave the beans out. Stir well.

7. It's also the time to mix in the **masa flour** for those that like an added flavor and their chili thicker (might have added too much spring water or gotten carried away with the beer). Mix the masa flour from both paks (2) with enough spring water to form a pourable mixture and stir enough into the chili to suit. A lot of folks don't use masa flour. If you'd rather have your chili without masa flour, leave it out (we try to please everyone).

8. Simmer for an additional 20-30 minutes or until the meat is good and tender. Add salt or crushed caliente red peppers to taste.

Now you're ready to enjoy **D. L. Jardine's Original Ranch House Chili**. There's simply none better!

Chapter Five

A Slavic Christmas

Just as the German immigrants left their mark on Texas culture, so did the Czechs. Around the turn of the century, a good number of Czechs immigrated from Moravia and Bohemia to the eastern and central regions of Texas, where a sizeable Czech population can still be found in rural communities. In fact, in certain communities Czech is the first language of some of the residents.

Czechs are known for their hard work and practicality, as well as for their love of festivities, especially during the Christmas season. Music, of course, is central to any celebration, and the accordion, an integral part of Czech polkas, had a surprisingly far-reaching influence on other ethnic groups throughout Texas, from the Creole's Zydeco music to the Tex-Mex and Cajun bands.

Christmas caroling was a popular custom in the early Czech communities. Today, the tradition is carried on throughout Texas by Czech choral groups that visit hospitals and convalescent homes. Incidentally, the popular Christmas carol "Good King Wenceslas" was based on the story of Duke Wenceslas, the martyred ruler of Bohemia in the tenth century. Written by an Englishman, the song relates the tale of a page who is kept from freezing to death by walking in the footsteps of "the good king."

Food always reflects the influence of any group. Kolaches, a traditional Czech pastry, are now favored across the state. Though available year-round, these fruit-filled sweets are a special treat at Christmas time. Gingerbread cookies are another Texas Czech favorite during the holidays.

As in many communities settled by Europeans, once in Texas the Czechs carried on the tradition of St. Nicholas, with December 6 — the Feast of St. Nicholas — marking the beginning of the Christmas season. According to Czech legend, St. Nicholas climbs down from heaven on a golden rope, accompanied by an angel and a devil. The angel records the good and bad deeds of children, while the devil carries a whip and rattles a chain to remind children who have been bad of the fate that will await them if they don't mend their ways.

Czechs conclude the holiday season on January 6, the Feast of the Epiphany, which commemorates the Wise Men's visit to the Christ Child. On this day, groups of boys, representing the Three Wise Men, dress in long white robes and go from home to home. Using chalk that has been blessed by a priest, they mark the doorways with the initials of the Wise Men—Kaspar, Melchior and Balthazar—and sing songs in the Wise Men's honor. Legend has it that their visit will bring good fortune to the inhabitants, who in return invite the boys in, offering them food and drink. In Texas the custom was generally restricted to churches rather than individual homes, but in recent years families have begun to revive the old custom.

Side Dishes

Dressing & Gravy for the Holidays

"I mix this popular Christmas recipe with my hands
so all the lumps of bread are mashed up."
Mildred L. Pietzsch, Roscoe

Dressing:

1 layer (9-inch cake pan) CORNBREAD, crumbled
12 slices WHITE BREAD, crumbled
1 lg. ONION, chopped
3 ribs CELERY, chopped
2 tsp. SALT
8 Tbsp. POULTRY SEASONING
2 cans (14 1/2 oz. ea.) CHICKEN or TURKEY BROTH
6 EGGS

Crumble cornbread and white bread. Add chopped onion and celery. Sprinkle salt and poultry seasoning over the mixture. Add broth a little at a time and stir well. Add eggs and mix well. If mixture is dry, add a little more broth reserving the balance for the gravy. Spray a 16 x 5 roasting pan, pour mixture into it and cover with lid or foil. Bake at 325 degrees for 2 1/2 hours. Serve with **Giblet Gravy**.

Serves 24.

Giblet Gravy:

3 1/2 cups TURKEY BROTH
1 tsp. SALT
3 EGGS, boiled
TURKEY LIVERS and GIZZARD, cooked and chopped
2 Tbsp. FLOUR for thickening

Add enough water to reserved broth from dressing to make 3 1/2 cups. Put broth in a 2-quart pan and bring to a boil. Add salt, chopped eggs, chopped liver and gizzard. Make a paste with 1/4 cup water and flour. Pour into boiling broth. Stir constantly until mixture begins to thicken.

Crunchy Pecan Broccoli

1 pkg. (16 oz.) FROZEN CHOPPED BROCCOLI
1 pkg. (10 oz.) FROZEN CAULIFLOWER
1/8 cup WATER
1 pkg. DRIED ONION SOUP MIX
3/4 stick MARGARINE, melted and divided
1/2 cup WATER
2/3 cup PECANS, chopped
1 can (5 oz.) sliced WATER CHESTNUTS, drained
3/4 cup CHEDDAR CHEESE, grated
2 1/2 cups RICE KRISPIES®, crushed

Place broccoli and cauliflower in a casserole dish with a lid. Add 1/8 cup water. Microwave for 6 minutes, stirring twice. (Or, cook lightly by conventional method). In a large mixing bowl, combine soup mix, half of the melted margarine, 1/2 cup water, pecans, water chestnuts and cheese; mix. Add the cooked, drained broccoli and cauliflower to the soup-pecan mixture. Toss and place in a greased 2 1/2-quart or a 9 x 13 greased baking dish. Add remaining margarine to the crushed Rice Krispies; mix. Top casserole with the Rice Krispies. Bake, uncovered, in a 350 degree oven for 25 minutes.

Serves 8-10.

Squash Dressing Casserole

"For my family, I double this recipe. It is always a big hit."
Helen Souther, Chico

1 cup ONION
1 cup CELERY
1 cup GREEN PEPPER
BUTTER
2 lb. YELLOW SQUASH, seasoned and cooked
1 pkg. CORNBREAD MIX, baked
2 cups MILK
1 can CREAM OF CHICKEN SOUP
1 tsp. SAGE
SALT and PEPPER to taste
1 cup SHREDDED CHEESE

In saucepan, sauté the onion, celery and green pepper in butter. Drain and mash cooked squash. Crumble the baked cornbread into the milk. Combine cornbread mixture, sautéed vegetables, cream of chicken soup and seasonings. Put all in greased casserole pan. Sprinkle 1 cup shredded cheese over top and bake 1 hour in a 350 degree oven. Serves 10.

Mary's Dressing

1/2 lb. SAUSAGE, browned
1 cup CELERY, finely chopped
1 cup ONION, finely chopped
10 cup CORNBREAD, crumbled
8 cups BISCUITS, crumbled
1 1/2 cups PECANS, chopped
1/2 tsp. SALT
2 tsp. POULTRY SEASONING
1/2 tsp. PEPPER
6 EGGS, beaten
4 to 5 cans CHICKEN BROTH

Brown sausage and sauté celery and onions together. Add to crumbled bread crumbs, pecans, seasonings, eggs and broth. Mix well. Bake at 350 degrees until done. You can use a food processor to chop all of the ingredients.

Sweet Potato Soufflé

3 cups canned, SWEET POTATOES, mashed
1 cup BROWN SUGAR
2 EGGS, beaten
1 can (5 oz.) EVAPORATED MILK
1/2 tsp. SALT
1 tsp. VANILLA

Combine above ingredients and pour into casserole or soufflé dish that has been lightly sprayed with cooking spray.

Topping:

1 cup BROWN SUGAR   **1/2 stick MARGARINE, melted**
1/2 cup FLOUR   **1 cup PECANS, finely chopped**

Mix topping ingredients and sprinkle over potatoes. Bake at 400 degrees for 30 to 40 minutes.

Serves 6-8.

Posole

Posole is a bean, meat and hominy soup. In Sonora, Mexico, posole has a chili soup base. Typically, posole is made with pork, but beef can also be used.

3 quarts WATER   **1 GARLIC CLOVE, minced**
2 cups PINTO BEANS   **1 BAY LEAF**
1 1/2 lbs. PORK, cut in   **1 Tbsp. SALT**
bite-sized pieces   **1/8 tsp. OREGANO**
1 small ONION, sliced in   **1 can (15 oz.) WHITE**
thin rings   **HOMINY, drained**

Bring water to a fast boil. Add all ingredients EXCEPT hominy. Cook, covered, over medium heat until beans and meat are tender (about 1 hour 25 minutes.) Add hot water in small amounts as needed during cooking. Remove bay leaf. During last 10 minutes of cooking, add hominy. Mix well.

Serves 6

Green Bean Olé

2 cans FRENCH CUT GREEN BEANS
1 cup SOUR CREAM
8 oz. VELVEETA® JALAPEÑO CHEESE, cut in chunks
1/2 ONION, minced
1/2 tsp. PEPPER
1 can WATER CHESTNUTS, drained and chopped
2 cups crushed CORNFLAKES or RICE KRISPIES®
3 Tbsp. MARGARINE, melted

Drain green beans well. Butter a 2 1/2-quart baking dish. In a large saucepan, melt the sour cream and cheese, stirring constantly. Add onion, pepper, water chestnuts, and green beans; mix. Pour into the buttered baking dish. Combine crushed cornflakes or Rice Krispies and margarine and sprinkle over green bean mixture and bake at 350 degrees for 30 minutes.

Serves 6-8.

Gazpacho

1 can (15 oz.) GARBANZO BEANS, drained
1 large CUCUMBER, peeled, sliced
2 large TOMATOES, peeled, chopped in small pieces
1 small GREEN PEPPER, seeded, sliced
3 cups boiling WATER
1 tsp. SALT
1/2 tsp. PEPPER
1 Tbsp. TABASCO® SAUCE (or other hot salsa)
1 small LIME, thinly sliced

In a serving bowl, combine garbanzos, cucumber slices, chopped tomatoes and green peppers.

To boiling water, add salt, pepper and Tabasco sauce or hot salsa. Blend thoroughly. Combine with garbanzo mixture and add sliced lime, let stand 5 minutes. Serve at room temperature or chilled.

Serves 4-5.

Cornbread Dressing

"This is what I make for every Christmas dinner of turkey and all the trimmings. I decided that it would be easier than making cornbread ahead of time for the dressing. This way it's all one process." Charlotte Myrick, Wellington

2 cups sautéed ONION and CELERY
2 cups CORNMEAL
1 Tbsp. SAGE
1 Tbsp. LEAF OREGANO
1/2 tsp. GARLIC POWDER
4 tsp. BAKING POWDER
1 1/2 tsp. SALT
4 EGGS
1 1/2 cup MILK
6 slices BREAD, crumbled
CHICKEN BROTH to make thick soupy mixture

Sauté onion and celery in butter until tender. Combine all ingredients and bake in a 9 x 13 pan at 350 degrees until firm—about 1 hour.

Shortcut Recipe:
1 cup ONION, chopped
1 cup CELERY, chopped
1/2 stick BUTTER or MARGARINE
2 pkg. CORNBREAD MIX
1 box or pkg. STUFFING MIX
4 EGGS
1 Tbsp. SAGE
1 Tbsp. LEAF OREGANO
1/2 tsp. GARLIC POWDER
BROTH and/or MILK to make thick soupy mixture

Sauté onion and celery in butter until tender. Combine all ingredients and bake at 350 degrees in 9 x 13 pan until firm.

Serves about 20.

Vegetable Medley

This goes well with Christmas ham and can be made the night before.

1 can FRENCH CUT GREEN BEANS
1 sm. can LESEUR® SWEET PEAS
1 can SHOE-PEG CORN (do not substitute)
1 cup ONION, chopped
1/4 cup CELERY, chopped
1/4 cup PIMENTOS
1 sm. can MUSHROOMS
1 cup VINEGAR
1 cup SUGAR
1/4 cup VEGETABLE OIL

Drain canned vegetables. Mix all vegetables in large bowl. Add vinegar, sugar and oil. Mix well. Refrigerate for several hours or overnight.

Hot Fruit

This is good as a side dish, but is especially tasty for brunch.

1 can (16 oz.) APRICOT HALVES, drained
1 can (16 oz.) PEAR HALVES, drained
1 can (16 oz.) SLICED PINEAPPLE, drained
1 can (15 1/2 oz.) PINEAPPLE CHUNKS, drained
1/2 cup MARGARINE
1/2 cup SUGAR
1 cup SHERRY
2 Tbsp. FLOUR
MARASCHINO CHERRIES, halved for garnish

Mix fruit and pour into baking dish. Melt margarine and add sugar, sherry and flour. Mix well. Cook 15 to 20 minutes or until slightly thickened. Pour over fruit and top with cherry halves. Bake at 350 degrees for 20 minutes.

Chapter Six

Christmas in Panna Maria

Texas was home to the first Polish settlement in the United States—Panna Maria in Karnes County. In 1854, Father Leopold Moczygemba and 100 families left the Upper Silesia region of Poland seeking religious freedom. They landed in Galveston and walked 200 miles to the junction of the San Antonio River and the Cibolo Creek. Arriving on Christmas Eve, they named their new home Panna Maria — the Virgin Mary. Two years later, the Church of the Immaculate Conception was ready for Midnight Mass. Panna Maria today has a population of approximately 100, many of whom still follow the traditions of their homeland culture.

Stars play an important role in Polish Christmas customs. On Christmas Eve, or Wigilia, the appearance of the first star of the evening sky—the Star of Bethlehem—signals the end of the day's fast and heralds the beginning of the feasting. Tradition calls for an odd number of dishes for the evening meal, ranging from five to thirteen, and an even number of diners. Empty place settings represent absent family members and the Christ Child. Straw is placed under the tablecloth as a reminder of the manger where Christ was born. Oplatki, small white wafers symbolizing the Sacred Host, are served at the meal. The food served comes from the fields, the orchards, the rivers and so forth, representing all the available sources of sustenance in the hopes that next year's harvest will be bountiful.

After the meal, Star Man arrives to quiz the children in catechism, giving a small token to each child. Star Man is accompanied by the Star Boys, who are costumed as nativity figures—the Wise Men, shepherds, even animals. When the festivities draw to a close, everyone heads to Midnight Mass, the Mass of the Shepherds, so named for the shepherds who first heard the news of the birth of the Christ Child.

On Christmas Day, families gather together for dinner. As it was in Poland, ham is the traditional favorite. Two other customary dishes, Polish sausage and dried mushrooms, usually find a place on the table alongside the best of Texas produce.

Annual Christmas festivities in Panna Maria include the singing of Polish Christmas carols and the lighting of the Christmas tree. As part of the *Christmas Along the Corridor* celebration, the village also welcomes a Pony Express courier en route from Presidio La Bahia in Goliad to Mission San Juan in San Antonio, the route of the first mail route in Spanish Colonial Texas.

Breads

Banana Nut Muffins

"Banana Nut Cake was one of the special cakes my mother made when I was young. It was a favorite of the entire family. I have changed her recipe to better fit our diet of today. We have these muffins for breakfast or after school snacks. I give them for Christmas gifts and have gotten lots of requests for the recipe." Elsie Pierce, Sweetwater

1 1/2 cups SUGAR
2/3 cup SHORTENING
4 EGGS WHITES
1 1/4 cups BANANAS, mashed
1 cup WHOLE WHEAT FLOUR
1 cup FLOUR
1/2 cup OATMEAL FLOUR (see note below)
1 1/4 tsp. BAKING POWDER
1 1/2 tsp. BAKING SODA
1 tsp. CINNAMON (optional)
2/3 cup BUTTERMILK (see note below)
1 1/2 tsp. VANILLA FLAVORING
2/3 cup NUTS, chopped

Preheat oven to 350 degrees. Cream shortening and sugar. Add egg whites, beating well. Add mashed banana. Blend. Add all three flours and baking powder, baking soda, cinnamon if desired, buttermilk and vanilla. Blend and then beat at medium speed for at least 2 minutes. Stir in chopped nuts. Spray 24 muffin or cupcake tins with cooking spray. Fill each cup 2/3 full and bake 25 to 30 minutes. Cool 5 minutes and remove from tins. Recipe can also be baked in 1-pound coffee cans for 45 minutes. Remove from can and cool completely. Put back in can for storage or freezing. Muffins freeze well, too.

Note: To make oatmeal flour, add 1 cup quick cooking oatmeal to food processor. Process until flour consistency (can be used for any recipe calling for flour.) To make buttermilk, add 1 tsp. vinegar to lowfat milk. Let stand 2 to 3 minutes.

Date-Nut Bread

This recipe can be made ahead and frozen, and you'll always have a dessert for unexpected company or a quick gift for the holidays.

1 cup DATES, chopped
1 cup HOT WATER
1/4 cup SHORTENING
3/4 cup BROWN SUGAR
1 EGG

1/2 cup PECANS, chopped
1 tsp. BAKING SODA
1/2 tsp. SALT
2 cups FLOUR

Let dates sit in hot water until soft. Cream shortening and sugar. Add egg, dates, pecans and dry ingredients. Mix well. Bake in greased and floured loaf pan for 50 to 60 minutes at 350 degrees.

Biscochuelos

Biscochuelos is a Mexican sweet bread. It makes an excellent after-dinner dessert with coffee! Serve with honey, butter or cream cheese.

3 cups FLOUR
1 1/2 Tbsp. BAKING POWDER
1 tsp. SALT
1/1/2 tsp. ground ANISE
1 1/2 tsp. ground NUTMEG

1 tsp. CINNAMON
1 cup SUGAR + 2 Tbsp.
  BROWN SUGAR
1 1/2 cups SHORTENING
2 Tbsp. HONEY

Mix first 6 ingredients in a large bowl, blend well. Cream sugars in shortening and add honey. Mix thoroughly, then add to dry ingredients. Make an elastic dough, knead and use small amounts of warm water to keep from sticking. Form a loaf and place in well-greased loaf pan. Bake at 350 degrees for 45 minutes or until bread is brown. Insert a bread knife in the middle of loaf to check for doneness. Make 5 "holes" in top of bread and add butter.

Makes 1 loaf.

Cranberry Coconut Coffee Cake

This is sure to be a hit at Christmas brunch and great for gift giving!

1 pkg. (18.25 oz) YELLOW CAKE MIX
1 pkg. (3.4 oz.) VANILLA INSTANT PUDDING
5 lg. EGGS
1/2 cup BOURBON
1/2 cup MILK
1/2 cup VEGETABLE OIL
2 cups fresh or frozen CRANBERRIES, chopped
1 cup PECANS, chopped
1 cup FLAKED COCONUT
Sifted POWDERED SUGAR

Combine first 6 ingredients in a large mixing bowl; beat at low speed with an electric mixer until smooth. Beat at high speed 3 minutes. Fold in cranberries, pecans and coconut. Pour mixture into a greased and floured Bundt pan. Bake at 350 degrees for 55 minutes or until a wooden pick inserted in center of cake comes out clean. Cool in pan on a wire rack 10 minutes. Remove from pan, and let cool completely on wire rack. Sprinkle with powdered sugar.

 # Pumpkin Bread

1 cup OIL	**1 tsp. CINNAMON**
5 EGGS	**1 tsp. NUTMEG**
2 cups PUMPKIN	**1 tsp. BAKING SODA**
2 cups SUGAR	**2 pkg. INSTANT COCONUT**
2 cups FLOUR	**or VANILLA PIE FILLING**
1 tsp. SALT	**1 cup PECANS**

Mix all ingredients well. Bake at 325 degrees for 1 hour or until done.

Coffee Can Bread

Try this unique way to make bread!

1 pkg. REGULAR GRANULATED
   YEAST (not rapid rise)
1/2 cup WARM WATER
1/4 tsp. ground GINGER
1 tsp. SUGAR
1/3 cup SUGAR

1 can (12-oz.) EVAPOR-
   ATED MILK
2 Tbsp. VEGETABLE OIL
1 tsp. SALT
4 1/4 cups FLOUR

Mix yeast, warm water, ginger and 1 teaspoon sugar in large bowl and let stand for 15 minutes. Add 1/3 cup sugar, evaporated milk, vegetable oil, salt and flour. Put into greased 2-pound coffee can. Grease plastic top and put on can. Let rise until the lid pops off. Remove top rack of oven. Leave can lid off. Bake at 350 degrees for 50 minutes. Cool in can for 10 minutes. Turn out on rack and cool completely. Store in can with top on. Great toasted.

Cranberry-Banana Bread

2 cups FLOUR
1 1/4 cups SUGAR
1 tsp. SALT
1 tsp. BAKING SODA
1 EGG, beaten
1/3 cup ORANGE JUICE (no pulp)
1/4 cup VEGETABLE OIL
2 Tbsp. WHITE VINEGAR
3/4 cup ripe BANANAS, mashed
1 1/4 cup CRANBERRIES, coarsely chopped
1 cup PECANS or WALNUTS, chopped

Mix dry ingredients. Combine egg, orange juice, vegetable oil, vinegar and add to flour mixture. Stir just until flour is moistened. Do not use electric mixer. Fold in bananas, cranberries and nuts. Pour into lightly oiled 9 x 5 x 3 loaf pan. Bake at 350 degrees for 60 to 70 minutes.

Pumpkin Muffins

Arrowhead Mills, Hereford

2 1/2 cups WHOLE WHEAT PASTRY FLOUR
1/2 cup WHEAT BRAN
3 tsp. non-alum BAKING POWDER
1 tsp. CINNAMON
1/2 tsp. NUTMEG
1/4 tsp. CLOVES
1 tsp. SEA SALT (optional)
1/2 cup NUTS, chopped
2 EGGS
1/4 cup unrefined SUNFLOWER OIL
1/2 cup HONEY
2 cups PUMPKIN PUREÉ
1 tsp. grated ORANGE RIND
1 cup RAISINS
1/2 cup pitted DATES, chopped

Combine dry ingredients. In a separate bowl, beat eggs and add oil, honey and pumpkin. Combine the two mixtures. Add orange rind, raisins and dates. Stir till all dry ingredients are moistened. Fill oiled muffin tins 2/3 full. Bake at 375 degrees for 30 minutes for large muffins or 20 minutes for mini-muffins. Allow to cool 5 minutes before removing from the pan.

Yield: 24 large or 48 mini-muffins.

Holiday Dinner Rolls

Arrowhead Mills, Hereford

2 tsp. DRY YEAST
3/4 cups warm WATER
1/4 cup HONEY
1/4 tsp. SEA SALT (optional)
1/4 cup VEGETABLE OIL plus enough WATER
    to make 1/3 cup liquid
1 EGG or EGG SUBSTITUTE
1/2 cup prepared POTATO FLAKES
1 1/2 cups WHOLE WHEAT FLOUR
2 cups unbleached WHITE FLOUR

Dissolve yeast in warm water in large bowl. Leave until bubbly, about 10 minutes. Add honey, salt, oil, egg, potatoes and half of the flour. Beat thoroughly. Add enough flour to make dough manageable. Turn out into lightly floured board and knead for 10 minutes until dough is smooth and elastic. Place in lightly oiled bowl, turning once to coat. Place in warm place and let rise for 1 hour. Punch down, turn onto floured board and shape into desired shape of roll. Place rolls on greased cookie sheet. Cover lightly with plastic or cotton towel and place in warm place to rise, about 20 to 30 minutes. Bake at 375 degrees for 15 to 20 minutes.

Chapter Seven

The Scandinavian Influence

In the late nineteenth century, Texas attracted a number of immigrants from the Scandinavian countries of Denmark, Norway and Sweden. Once settled in their new country they maintained many of the Christmas traditions from their homeland.

Many of the Scandinavian Christmas customs that were transported to Texas can trace their roots back to pagan times. The Swedish "Julbock", or Christmas goat, is a Christmas character that evolved from Norse mythology. "Thor", the god of thunder, rode upon a goat. Somehow, throughout the course of history, the goat became the mode of transportation for "Jultomten" on Christmas Eve. Jultomten is an elf who lives in a hayloft and protects the inhabitants of the home. Like Santa Claus, he delivers presents on Christmas Eve. He has a red cape and a white beard and rides in a sleigh, but instead of reindeer, Jultomten's sleigh is drawn by a goat—the Julbock. The Julbock has become a popular symbol of Christmas, and straw likenesses are frequently seen at Christmas fairs throughout Texas.

The custom of kissing beneath mistletoe also has its roots in Norse mythology. According to legend, "Balder", one of the best-loved Norse gods, dreamed that his life was in danger. His mother, "Frigga", vowed to protect him and went to all things—plants, trees, rocks—asking that they not harm her son. It became great fun for all the gods to playfully throw deadly objects at Balder since they knew that the object would live up to its promise to Frigga and not harm her son. Frigga, however, had overlooked the lowly mistletoe. When "Loki" a god who was jealous of Balder learned of Frigga's oversight, he tricked "Hoder", Balder's brother into throwing the mistletoe at Balder. The mistletoe pierced Balder's heart and he died instantly. Frigga realized that Loki, not the mistletoe, was responsible for Balder's death, and so she blessed the plant, declaring it a symbol of love, and promised that all who passed beneath its shiny green leaves would receive a kiss. How mistletoe became connected with Christmas has been forgotten over the ages, but mistletoe is big business for Texas, which produces ninety-five percent of the world's supply.

Another interesting Scandinavian custom is the "Julklapp", or Christmas box. A knock on the door or a window signals the arrival of a mystery present. After tossing the gift into the house, the giver hurries away before his identity can be discovered. The gift itself is something of a puzzle as it may be wrapped in layers of paper or hidden in a series of boxes. To heighten the sense of mystery, some gift givers provide only a clue to where the gift is hidden.

Although the exact origin of the Yule log is unknown, one theory holds that it began as a tribute to Thor. A huge log, known as the juul (pronounced yule), was burned in his honor during the winter solstice. With the transition to Christianity, the tradition became incorporated into Christmas celebrations. Various rituals surround the Yule log; each year it must be lit by a piece of the previous year's log and it must burn for the twelve days of Christmas.

Desserts

Cherry Cream Pie

"This cherry pie recipe is a must at Christmas time. When our youngest daughter married, our son-in-law let it be known that he did not like pies. When our first grandbaby was born, I fixed this pie and took it to their home. My son-in-law ate the whole pie. Now, this is the only dessert he wants our daughter to make." Mary Foster, Wellington.

1 can SOUR PITTED CHERRIES
2 cups WHIPPING CREAM
1 can SWEETENED CONDENSED MILK
1/3 cup LEMON JUICE
1 cup PECANS or WALNUTS, chopped
2 GRAHAM CRACKER PIE CRUSTS

Drain cherries and chop or cut in small pieces. Whip the 2 cups of whipping cream in a large bowl. Add the sweetened condensed milk, lemon juice, cherries and chopped nuts. Using mixer, blend well and pour into the graham cracker pie crusts. Cover and refrigerate until set.

Leche Quemada

This is a thick, dark caramel-colored pudding

8 cups MILK
2 cups SUGAR
1 cup blanched ALMONDS, ground

2 CINNAMON STICKS
1/4 cup SHERRY

Mix one cup milk and the sugar in a large, heavy saucepan. Cook over medium heat, stirring constantly, until sugar caramelizes to a light golden color. Add the remaining seven cups of milk, almonds and cinnamon sticks. Bring to a boil. Continue to boil, stirring occasionally, until thick and mixture forms a ribbon when poured from a spoon (about two hours). Add sherry and heat two or three minutes longer. Pour into individual dishes and cool. Serves 8.

Texas is one of the largest producers of pecans. The following recipes for Betty Ann's Best Pecan Pie and Never Fail Pie Crust — are provided courtesy of San Saba Pecan, Inc.

Known worldwide for its pecans, San Saba is an agricultural center, producing wool, mohair, cattle, horse, hogs, poultry and of course, pecans. This small town of roughly 2,600 was founded on the banks of the San Saba River in 1854.

Betty Ann's Best Pecan Pie

1/2 cup SUGAR
3 EGGS
1 cup WHITE CORN SYRUP
1 Tbsp. MELTED BUTTER
1 to 2 cups (as desired) SHELLED PECANS
2 Tbsp. FLOUR
1 tsp. VANILLA

Mix all ingredients, pour into unbaked pie shell, and bake 15 minutes in 400 degree oven. Then bake until set in 350 degree oven, approximately 45 minutes.

Never Fail Pie Crust

3 cups FLOUR
1 cup SHORTENING
1 tsp. SALT
1/2 cup HOT WATER

Mix all ingredients well. Roll into circles and then individually roll out dough to fit into pie pans. This recipe will make approximately three 10-inch pie crusts.

Christmas Sweet Potato Pie

Amber Combs, Seven Points

1 DEEP DISH PIE CRUST
3 cups SWEET POTATOES,
   cooked and mashed
1 cup SUGAR
2 EGGS
1/2 cup BUTTER, softened

1/2 tsp. NUTMEG
1/4 tsp. SALT
1 cup HALF & HALF
1 cup PECANS, chopped
1/2 cup RED and GREEN
   CANDIED CHERRIES

Preheat oven to 375 degrees. In a medium bowl, beat sweet potatoes until smooth and add sugar, eggs, butter, nutmeg, salt and half & half. Pour filling into uncooked pie shell to 1/2 inch from top of crust. Sprinkle nuts on top. Bake for 60 to 70 minutes or until a knife inserted in center of pie comes out clean. Sprinkle red and green candied cherries over nuts. Let cool completely before cutting. Serves 6 - 8.

Double Choco-Cherry Cake

"I experimented with this cake for my best friend's husband who loves chocolate. His birthday is December 22nd, and I make it for him then, just in time for Christmas!" Dorothy Geroianni, San Antonio

1 pkg. DARK CHOCOLATE CAKE MIX
1 can (21 oz.) CHERRY PIE FILLING
1 pkg. (12 oz.) SEMI-SWEET CHOCOLATE CHIPS

Prepare cake mix according to directions on package. Pour into a greased and floured 9 x 13 pan. Spoon cherry pie filling over cake mix and swirl through. Add 1/2 of the chocolate chips to batter and swirl again. Bake as directed on cake mix package. While still warm, sprinkle remaining chocolate chips over cake; the chips will melt—spread over top of cake while warm. Cool cake and serve.

Double Layer Pumpkin Pie

"My holiday guests always request this pie. It has all the usual ingredients and a few delectable extras that make it a real topper. Preparation time is only 15 minutes plus refrigeration time." Helen Ruetten, Elm Mott

Crust:
20-22 squares HONEY FLAVORED GRAHAM CRACKERS
2 Tbsp. SUGAR
6 Tbsp. BUTTER OR MARGARINE, melted

Crush crackers with rolling pin on wax paper. Combine with remaining ingredients in mixing bowl, stirring to blend well. Press mixture firmly in a 9-inch pie plate. Bake at 350 degrees for 8 minutes. Cool before filling.

Filling:
1 pkg. (3 oz.) CREAM CHEESE, softened
1 Tbsp. HALF & HALF
1 Tbsp. SUGAR
1 1/2 cups WHIPPED TOPPING, thawed
1 cup cold HALF & HALF
2 pkg. (4 serving size) VANILLA FLAVOR INSTANT PUDDING
1 can (16 oz.) PUMPKIN
1 tsp. ground CINNAMON
1/2 tsp. ground GINGER
1/4 tsp. ground CLOVES

Mix softened cream cheese, 1 tablespoon half & half and sugar until smooth. Gently stir in whipped topping. Spread on bottom of crust. Pour 1 cup half & half into mixing bowl. Add pudding mix and beat with wire whisk 1 to 2 minutes until well blended. Let stand 5 minutes or until thickened. Stir in pumpkin and spices and mix well. Spread over cream cheese layer. Refrigerate 2 hours or overnight. Garnish with additional whipped topping and chocolate dipped pecan halves, if desired.

Serves 8.

Buñuelos

Buñuelos are quick-fried fritters topped by a brown sugar syrup. They are round, thin and crispy!

2 cups FLOUR
3/4 tsp. SALT
4 Tsp. SHORTENING
2/3 cup WATER

Combine flour and salt. Mix in shortening. Add water a little at a time to make a soft dough. Knead for 5 minutes and form 9 dough balls. On a lightly-floured cutting board, use a rolling pin to roll out round, thin, sheets of dough. Quick-fry in hot oil, drain, then top with syrup.
Makes 9 buñuelos.

Miel (syrup) for Buñuelos

2 cups light BROWN SUGAR
2 cups WATER
1 to 2 CINNAMON STICKS

In a saucepan, dissolve sugar in water evenly. Bring to a fast boil, then reduce heat. Stir frequently. Remove cover and cook over medium heat for 15 minutes more until thickened. Pour into serving container with cinnamon sticks. Leave sticks in syrup for 10 to 15 minutes, then remove before serving.

Fruit Salad Pie

"I invented this pie as an alternative to rich Christmas pies. It is decorative and delicious." Marian Ramsay, Fort Worth

1 baked 9-INCH PIE SHELL
1 container (12 oz.) FROZEN STRAWBERRIES IN SUGAR
2 Tbsp. CORNSTARCH
2 drops RED FOOD COLORING
2 sm. TART APPLES, peeled and chopped
2 ORANGES, sectioned
2 sm. BANANAS, chopped
1 container WHIPPED TOPPING, thawed
1 KIWI FRUIT, peeled and sliced

Thaw the strawberries. Heat in saucepan with the cornstarch and food coloring until thickened. Cool to warm. Add the apples, oranges and bananas. Pour the mixture into the pie shell. Refrigerate 2 hours until cool. Cover the top of the pie with the defrosted topping. Slice the kiwi fruit and decorate the top of the pie. Return to refrigerator.

Pastel de Jicama y Piña

This jicama and pineapple pie will really get attention!

2 cups stewed JICAMA, diced
1 cup fresh PINEAPPLE, cubed
1/4 cup FLOUR
1 1/4 cups LIGHT BROWN SUGAR
1 Tbsp. LEMON JUICE
2 Tbsp. BUTTER
dash SALT
1/4 tsp. CINNAMON, ground
9" PASTRY SHELL

In a shallow cooking pot, combine jicama and pineapple. Add flour, brown sugar and lemon juice. Blend well. Add butter, salt and cinnamon. Heat until bubbly. Cover and let simmer 15 minutes. Cool. Pour into pastry shell and add "lattice" strips to top. Bake for 10 minutes at 425 degrees then 30 minutes at 350 degrees. Serve warm.

Mascarpone Tart with Fresh Fruit Topping

SWEET TART CRUST or SUGAR COOKIE DOUGH
1 lb. MASCARPONE
1/4 cup SUGAR
2 to 4 Tbsp. GRAND MARNIER® LIQUEUR
FRESH SLICED FRUITS and BERRIES
1/4 cup FRUIT JELLY

Make a sweet pastry crust or sugar cookie dough. Roll out and place in a tart pan. Bake until golden. Cool crust. Mix mascarpone with sugar and Grand Marnier. Spread mascarpone on tart crust. Arrange berries and/or sliced fruit over filling. Simmer jelly with about 1 Tbsp. Grand Marnier until thickened. Drizzle or paint glaze over fruit. Chill until about 30 minutes before serving.

Serves 6 to 8.

Chocolate Fudge Pie

"This always goes over big for the holidays. There is never any left over." Della Brown, Decatur

4 cups MILK
6 Tbsp. COCOA
2 cups + 5 Tbsp. SUGAR
5 EGGS, separated
4 Tbsp. BUTTER
10 Tbsp. FLOUR
2 tsp. VANILLA
2 baked 9-inch PIE SHELLS

Mix all ingredients except egg whites and 5 tablespoons sugar in heavy sauce pan. Cook until thick. Stir constantly. Pour into baked pie shells while hot. Beat egg whites and add 5 tablespoons of sugar. Spread on top of filling. Bake in 400 degree oven until golden brown.

Black Forest Cherry Cake

Rhonda Richey, Chico

1 CHOCOLATE CAKE MIX

Syrup:
- 3/4 cup SUGAR
- 1 cup WATER
- 1/3 cup CHERRY JUICE

Filling and topping:
- 1/2 cup POWDERED SUGAR
- 1/4 cup MARASCHINO CHERRY JUICE
- 1 cup MARASCHINO CHERRIES, chopped
- 3 cups WHIPPING CREAM, chilled or 1 lg. COOL WHIP®
- 4 to 6 oz. SEMI SWEET BAKING CHOCOLATE
- 6 to 12 canned CHERRIES WITH STEMS, well drained

Prepare cake mix as directed and bake in three 8-inch pans. To make syrup, combine sugar, water and cherry juice in saucepan; bring to a boil, stirring until sugar is dissolved. Boil 5 minutes. Remove from heat and let stand until lukewarm. Transfer cake layers to wax paper. Poke with fork several times. Drizzle syrup over layers and let set 5 minutes. To make icing, stir powdered sugar, cherry juice and chopped maraschino cherries into whipped cream. Place one layer on plate; spread top with 1/2-inch icing. Repeat with remaining layers, using remaining icing to cover top and sides. To decorate, make chocolate curls with carrot peeler and add stemmed cherries. Refrigerate until ready to serve.

Grandma's Red Christmas Cake

"We couldn't have a good Christmas dinner without my Red Christmas Cake. My family loves it. I've been making it for over sixty years." Vernie Bailey, Kemp

1 1/2 cups SHORTENING	2 1/4 cups FLOUR
1 1/2 sups SUGAR	1 tsp. SALT
2 EGGS	1 cup BUTTERMILK
2 bottles (1 oz.) RED	1 tsp. VANILLA
FOOD COLORING	1 Tbsp. VINEGAR
2 Tbsp. COCOA	1 tsp. BAKING SODA

Cream shortening and sugar in mixing bowl. Add eggs and beat until light and fluffy. Mix red food coloring and cocoa and add to sugar mixture. Beat well and add flour and salt alternately with buttermilk and vanilla. Add vinegar and baking soda. Mix until well blended. Divide batter into two 9-inch greased and floured pans. Bake 30 minutes at 350 degrees. Cool.

Frosting

3 Tbsp. CORNSTARCH	1/4 cup GREEN and RED
1 1/4 cups MILK	CANDIED CHERRIES,
1 cup SUGAR	chopped
1 cup SHORTENING	1/2 cup PECANS, chopped
1 tsp. VANILLA	

Mix cornstarch with 1/4 cup milk. Add remaining milk and cook over medium heat until thick. Pour into shallow plate and cover with plastic wrap so a crust will not form and refrigerate until cold. Mix sugar and shortening and add vanilla. Mix until very light. Add cornstarch-milk mixture and continue mixing until blended. Split each cake layer and frost between three layers. Top cake with remaining frosting, chopped cherries and pecans.

My Favorite Fruitcake

"I love this recipe because I am a lover of pecans and candied cherries and pineapple. Great with a hot cup of cocoa." Lucille Garcia, Beeville

3/4 cup BROWN SUGAR
1/2 cup MARGARINE or BUTTER
1 EGG
2 1/2 cups FLOUR
1 tsp. BAKING SODA
1/4 tsp. NUTMEG
1/4 tsp. CLOVES
1/2 tsp. CINNAMON
1 cup APPLESAUCE
1/4 cup ORANGE JUICE
1 cup CANDIED CHERRIES, cut into small pieces
1 cup CANDIED PINEAPPLE, cut into small pieces
2 cups PECAN PIECES

Cream sugar and margarine or butter. Add egg, beating well. Mix flour with spices and baking soda. Stir flour mixture into creamed mixture, alternately, with applesauce and juice. Fold in fruits and pecans. Pour into greased and floured 7 1/2 x 3 1/2 x 2 loaf pans. Bake for 1 hour at 325 degrees. Use the toothpick method to see if it is done in the middle. If desired, glaze fruitcake with a mixture of powdered sugar and juice and decorate with cherry halves. Can be frozen until needed.

Pumpkin Cake

"This makes a large cake for big groups; it also adds spice to the holidays but it is not too sweet. I thought up this recipe one fall when I had a large crop of pumpkin and wanted something different for church dinners. In all the times I took this cake, I never brought any back home!" Vivian Gaines, Clarksville

1 1/2 cups SUGAR
1/2 cup SHORTENING
1 cup PEANUT BUTTER
4 EGGS, beaten
2 cups COOKED PUMPKIN or 1 can (16 oz.) pumpkin
3 cups UNSIFTED FLOUR
1 tsp. SALT
1 tsp. PUMPKIN PIE SPICE
3 tsp. BAKING POWDER

Cream sugar, shortening, peanut butter; add beaten eggs and pumpkin and mix well. Combine flour, salt, spice and baking powder, and then add to first mixture. Beat with beater till smooth. Grease and flour two 9 x 13 cake pans and heat oven to 350 degrees. Pour batter in pans and bake on top rack for 20 to 30 minutes until done. Cool in pan or on rack.

Caramel Icing

2 cups BROWN SUGAR
1 cup POWDERED SUGAR
1 stick MARGARINE

Cream sugar and margarine and add enough water to make a paste. Spread over cooled cake layers.

Dan's Fruitcake

"Unlike other fruitcakes that have to age before being eaten, this cake is delicious eaten while still warm." Fran Forbes, Pleasanton

1 cup CANDIED CHERRIES	2 cups SUGAR
1 cup CANDIED PINEAPPLE	3 cups FLOUR
6 EGGS, separated	5 cups PECANS, chopped
2 cups BUTTER	2 oz. LEMON EXTRACT

Cut cherries and pineapple into small pieces. Separate eggs. Beat egg whites until stiff and set aside. Cream butter and sugar until creamy. Add egg yolks one at a time. In a separate bowl, put 1/2 cup flour and chopped fruits and nuts; mix gently. Into the butter and sugar mixture, add the remainder of the flour and lemon extract. Lastly, fold in the stiffly beaten egg whites and fruit/nut mixture. Bake in large Bundt pan at 325 degrees for 1 1/2 hours or until cake tester comes out clean.

Mother's Christmas Date Nut Cake

"This is a fruitcake for those who do not like citron. It's much easier to make as the fruits and nuts are left whole." Jody Feldtman Wright, San Antonio

1 lb. WALNUTS, shelled	1 tsp. BAKING POWDER
1/2 lb. PECANS, shelled	1/2 tsp. SALT
1/4 lb. CHERRIES	1 cup SUGAR
2 lb. DATES	4 EGGS
1 cup FLOUR	1 tsp. VANILLA

Leave fruits and nuts whole. Sift baking powder, salt and flour three times. Mix with fruits and nuts. Add sugar and mix well. Beat eggs separately. Mix in yolks, and then whites. Add vanilla. Bake in lined greased tube pan for 1 hour at 300-325 degrees.

Best Texas Chocolate Cake

2 cups FLOUR
2 cups SUGAR
1 stick BUTTER or MARGARINE
3 to 4 Tbsp. COCOA
1 cup WATER
1/2 cup SHORTENING
1/2 cup BUTTERMILK
1 tsp. BAKING SODA
2 EGGS
1 tsp. VANILLA

Preheat oven to 375 degrees. Mix sugar and flour together in mixing bowl. Heat butter, cocoa, water and shortening in a saucepan until it reaches boiling point. Pour hot mixture over the dry ingredients and add buttermilk with soda, eggs and vanilla. Mix well. Pour into greased and floured pan and bake for 20 to 25 minutes.

Icing

1 stick MARGARINE
3 Tbsp. COCOA
6 Tbsp. MILK
1 box POWDERED SUGAR
1 tsp. VANILLA
1/2 cup NUTS, chopped

Put margarine, cocoa and milk in saucepan and heat until almost boiling. Remove from heat and add powdered sugar. Beat well and add vanilla and nuts. Pour over hot cake. You can also add coconut.

Texas Pecan Cake

3/4 lb. BUTTER or MARGARINE
3 cups SUGAR
6 EGGS, separated
2 oz. LEMON EXTRACT, or 1/2 cup WINE and
    2 tsp. VANILLA
3 cups FLOUR
1 qt. PECANS, chopped
1/2 lb. RED CANDIED CHERRIES, chopped
1/2 lb. CANDIED PINEAPPLE, chopped

Cream butter and sugar. Add egg yolks one at a time, mixing well after each addition. Add lemon extract. Add flour, nuts, cherries and pineapple. Beat egg whites and fold in, mixing well. Pour into a well-greased and floured tube pan and bake at 225 degrees for 3 hours.

Texas Delight

1/2 cup BUTTER or MARGARINE
1 cup FLOUR
1/2 cup PECANS
1 cup POWDERED SUGAR
1 container (8 oz.) WHIPPED TOPPING
1 pkg. (8 oz.) CREAM CHEESE, softened
2 pkg. (3 5/8 oz.) instant CHOCOLATE PUDDING
2 1/2 cups MILK
PECANS, chopped for garnish

Melt butter in oblong baking dish. Mix in flour and pecans. Bake 15 minutes at 350 degrees. Cool. Mix powdered sugar, half of the whipped topping and the cream cheese. Spread over cooled crust. Mix pudding with milk and beat. Pour over cheese layer and top with remainder of whipped topping. Garnish with chopped pecans. Chill several hours.

Serves 15.

White Christmas Cake

4 EGG WHITES
1 1/2 cups SUGAR, divided
2 cups plus 2 Tbsp. ALL-PURPOSE FLOUR
3 1/2 tsp. BAKING POWDER
1/2 cup VEGETABLE SHORTENING
1 cup MILK
1 1/2 tsp. ALMOND EXTRACT
2/3 cup FLAKED COCONUT

Preheat oven to 350 degrees. Beat egg whites until foamy. Gradually beat in 1/2 cup of sugar and continue beating until stiff peaks form. Set aside. In mixing bowl, combine remaining 1 cup sugar, flour, baking powder and salt. Add shortening, milk and almond extract. Beat 30 seconds on low speed of electric mixer; scrape bowl. Beat 2 minutes longer on medium speed. Gently fold in beaten egg whites and coconut. Spread batter in two greased and floured 9 inch layer pans. Bake for 30-35 minutes or until cake tests done. Cool 10 minutes before removing from pan. Cool completely. Frost with white frosting and garnish with additional coconut.

Cherry Cake

"This recipe can be made with chocolate cake mix, or with spice cake mix and apple pie filling. A very good cake, and the icing is delicious!" Pam Cole, Holiday

1 DUNCAN HINES® STRAWBERRY SUPREME CAKE MIX
3 EGGS
1 tsp. LEMON EXTRACT
1 can CHERRY PIE FILLING

Mix cake mix, eggs and lemon extract. Add pie filling. Bake in three 8-inch cake pans at 350 degrees for 30 to 35 minutes. Cool.

Icing

1 cup SOUR CREAM
1 1/2 cups SUGAR
1 lg. container (12 oz.) WHIPPED TOPPING
COCONUT, shredded

Mix first three ingredients together. Ice the three layers, covering top and sides. Then cover with coconut. Let set in refrigerator for 3 days.

Apple Cranberry Casserole

2 cups CRANBERRIES
3 cups APPLES, sliced
   and peeled
1 cup SUGAR
1 Tbsp. LEMON JUICE
1/4 tsp. SALT

1 cup QUICK COOKING
   OATS
1/2 cup FLOUR
1 cup BROWN SUGAR
1/3 cup MARGARINE

Combine cranberries, apples, sugar, lemon juice and salt. Pour into 1 1/2-quart baking dish. Combine oats, flour, brown sugar and margarine. Spread over fruit. Bake at 325 for 1 hour. Serve warm.

Ambrosia Marmalade

"When I was a child in Alabama, I remember my mother serving ambrosia and pound cake at Christmas time. When I married and came to Texas to live, I made this recipe up in order to have ambrosia all year round. This is a rich marmalade, good on hot buttered biscuits or as a topping for cake or ice cream." Myrtle Thomas, Clarksville

1 can (46 oz.) ORANGE JUICE
1 can (46 oz.) PINEAPPLE JUICE
1 pt. bottle MARASCHINO CHERRIES and JUICE
2 cans (20 oz.) CRUSHED PINEAPPLE
1 can FLAKED COCONUT
10 lb. SUGAR
3 boxes SURJELL® (regular cooking)

In a large jelly kettle, mix fruit juices, maraschino cherries (cut in half), pineapple and coconut. Add Surjell and mix well until dissolved. Bring to a rolling boil and add sugar. Stir till sugar is dissolved and bring to a boil again; cook 3 minutes. Ladle into sterilized pint jars. Wipe jar tops clean, cap and seal jars, and process 5 minutes in boiling water bath.

Sugarplum Rice Pudding

A Scandinavian holiday delicacy for Texas tables.

2 cups MILK
2/3 cup SUGAR
1/4 tsp. SALT
1/4 cup FLOUR
1 tsp. VANILLA
1/2 tsp. CINNAMON
2 EGGS, beaten
1/3 cup CURRANTS, plumped in
    warm water and drained
1/2 cup PINEAPPLE PRESERVES
2 1/2 cups COOKED RICE
1/4 cup MARASCHINO CHERRIES, slivered
1/3 cup FLAKED COCONUT
1/3 cup NUTS, chopped
WHIPPED CREAM (optional)
CANDIED RED and GREEN CHERRIES (optional)

Heat milk to boiling over moderate heat; remove from heat. Mix sugar, salt and flour; quickly but thoroughly stir into milk. Return to heat and bring to a boil. Stir vanilla and cinnamon into beaten eggs; stir small amount of hot mixture into egg mixture; then pour egg mixture back into pudding, stirring over heat until thickened. Blend in currants, pineapple preserves, rice, cherries, coconut and nuts. Chill. If desired, serve in parfait glasses, topped with whipped cream and garnished with candied red and green cherries.

Chapter Eight

The Many Faces of a Texas Christmas

Christmas, perhaps more so than any other holiday, is a time for remembering one's heritage. One of the things that makes Christmas in Texas unique is that the state's diverse heritage encourages a mingling of various religious and ethnic cultures. A celebration that embodies this intermingling of traditions is the *Feast of the Virgin of Guadalupe*, a Roman Catholic holiday honoring the Virgin Mary, in which Catholic, Indian and Hispanic traditions combine in a unique celebration.

The *Feast of the Virgin of Guadalupe* on December 12 commemorates the appearance of the Virgin Mary to an Indian who had converted to Catholicism. Throughout Texas and the Southwest, this day is celebrated with the "matachine", an ancient Indian folk dance. In many towns and villages, dancers form a procession to the local church. As the procession, headed by a large cross decorated with flowers, makes its way toward the church, dancers, dressed in red velveteen coats adorned with ornaments and bells, are accompanied by musicians playing violins, drums, accordions and guitars. As its citizens have preserved a variation of the dance that has been lost in other cities in the Southwest and Mexico, the town of Laredo is especially renown for its matachine procession.

Another celebration that bonds ethnic and cultural traditions is the Ethiopian festival of "Kwanza". Kwanza is an ancient festival that was rediscovered as African-Americans sought a connection with their past. The celebration was introduced to the United States about 30 years ago, and has been celebrated by families in the urban areas of Texas for several years, but has been relatively unknown among the general public until recently. Kwanza, which means "first fruits" or "harvest", features a week of celebration, from December 26 to January 1. It is a time of purification of the mind, body and soul. During the week-long celebration, a candle is lit each day symbolizing one of seven principles that can be used to improve life: unity, self-determination, collective work and responsibility, cooperative economics, purposes, creativity and faith. Born out of a desire to preserve ancient traditions, celebrations such as these make Christmas in Texas one of the most wonderful times of the year.

Cookies, Candies & Bars

Aunt Bill's Candy

Jo Ann Tucker, Chico

6 cups SUGAR
2 cups CREAM or EVAPORATED MILK
1 Tbsp. WHITE CORN SYRUP
1/4 tsp. BAKING SODA
1/2 cup BUTTER or MARGARINE
1 tsp. VANILLA
2 cups PECANS, chopped

Caramelize 2 cups sugar by melting it in a heavy skillet. Combine 4 cups sugar with cream and corn syrup in a large saucepan. Bring to a boil while sugar is caramelizing. Pour caramelized sugar slowing into boiling mixture, stirring constantly. Cook to 245 degrees, stirring frequently. Remove from heat and immediately add baking soda, stirring vigorously as mixture foams up. Add butter and stir until melted. Cool 20 minutes. Add vanilla and beat until thick and creamy. Add pecans. Pour into buttered 9 x 13 pan. Cool and cut into squares.

Yield: 4 pounds.

A variation:

Divide the mixture after adding the butter. Add pecans to one half, coconut to the other. Instead of pouring the mixture into a pan drop by teaspoonful onto wax paper.

Cowboy Cookies

Florence Belzung of San Antonio, declares "It would not be Christmas without Cowboy Cookies." Over the years she has revised the recipe, adding new ingredients.

1 cup WHITE SUGAR
1 cup DARK BROWN SUGAR
1 cup SHORTENING
2 EGGS
1 tsp. VANILLA
1 1/2 cups FLOUR
1 tsp. BAKING SODA
1 tsp. BAKING POWDER
1 tsp. SALT
2 cups CORNFLAKES
1/2 cup QUICK COOKING OATS
1 1/2 cup FLAKED COCONUT
1 cup CHOCOLATE CHIPS
1/2 cup PECANS, chopped

Cream sugars and shortening. Blend in eggs and vanilla. Sift flour, baking soda, baking powder and salt together; add to creamed mixture. Stir in cornflakes, oats, coconut, chocolate chips and pecans. Drop from teaspoon to greased cookie sheets. Bake at 350 degrees for 12 minutes.

Yield: Approximately 6 dozen.

The Ervendberg Orphanage & the Timmermann Sisters

An old-fashioned German Christmas can be experienced at the home of the Timmermann sisters in the small town of Geronimo, near Seguin. The sisters are famous for their annual Christmas display in their nineteenth century seven-gabled farmhouse built by their family. Four of them have passed away, but the remaining three sisters, now in their eighties, carry on the family traditions, as they have for the last 70 years. The Timmermann sisters' celebration can trace its roots back to the 1840s, when Louis C. Ervendberg, the sisters' great-grand-father, opened his heart and his home to 19 orphans. At Christmas time, the focal point of the Ervendberg home and orphanage was its magnificent Christmas tree, with an elaborate nativity scene beneath its branches. In 1849, Herman Seele, a Christmas visitor from nearby New Braunfels, was so impressed with the beautiful decorations and the well-behaved children that he recorded his impressions. Today, the sisters recreate the scene so vividly described in Seele's book. And like their great grandfather before them, the Timmermann sisters open their home to holiday visitors—as many as 1500 guests each year behold their tree, nativity scene and a replica of the orphanage.

Theeletterchen An Den Weinachsbaum

(Sugar Cookies)

This recipe for sugar cookies was handed down from the Timmermann sisters' great-grandmother. Delicious as well as functional, these cookies can be hung on the tree and Wanda Timmermann promises "they will not fall from the tree during moist drizzly weather."

3 1/2 cups SUGAR　　　　**3 EGGS**
1 cup BUTTER　　　　　　**4 cups FLOUR**

Preheat oven to 350 degrees. Cream butter and sugar until light and creamy. Add eggs, beating well after each egg is added. Stir in flour. Wrap in waxed paper and chill 1 to 2 hours. Roll on floured surface to a scant 1/4-inch thickness. Cut with your favorite cookie cutter. Make a hole in cookie if you plan to hang them on the tree. Bake 12 to 15 minutes. Cool on rack and decorate at your convenience. Yield: Approximately 3 1/2 dozen.

Sugar Coated Peanuts

"We always have these on Christmas Eve. I am now 66 years old, and I don't think the peanuts have missed a Christmas." Melba Mullen, Steelville

1 lb. RAW PEANUTS
1 cup SUGAR
1 cup WATER

Preheat oven to 350 degrees. Place all ingredients in a bowl and mix well. Pour on cookie sheet and bake 30 to 35 minutes or until dry. Cool before serving.

Sandra's Fruitcake Cookies

"This is a must at Christmas time. Most of the time, I double the recipe." Sandra Davis, Holiday

PINCH OF SALT
1 1/2 cup FLOUR
2 EGGS
1/2 tsp. CINNAMON
1 lb. DATES, chopped
1 lb. PECANS, chopped
1 1/2 tsp. BAKING SODA

1/2 cup BROWN SUGAR
1 stick MARGARINE
1 tsp. VANILLA
1 JAR (8 oz.) CHERRIES,
    drained & chopped
1 1/2 Tbsp. MILK

Mix all ingredients and drop by teaspoonful on greased cookie sheet. Bake at 325 degrees for 12 to 15 minutes.

Buttermilk Fudge

1 cup BUTTERMILK
1 tsp. BAKING SODA
1/4 cup BUTTER
2 Tbsp. CORN SYRUP
2 cups SUGAR

1 tsp. VANILLA
1 cup COCONUT
1 1/2 cups PECANS,
    chopped

Add soda to buttermilk. Let stand 1 minute. Mix buttermilk and soda with butter, corn syrup, sugar and vanilla in large pan. Cook on high heat to boil. Lower to medium heat and cook to soft-ball stage. Stir occasionally. Remove from heat and let stand 5 minutes. Beat until creamy. Add coconut and pecans. Drop onto waxed paper. This is similar to creamy pralines.

Peanut Patties

"This recipe makes one of the best peanut patties that I have ever eaten. I have been asked to make this for Christmas open house. The townspeople always say that they know who made this candy." Mary Foster, Wellington

2/3 cup CORN SYRUP
2 1/2 cups SUGAR
1/2 pint WHIPPING CREAM
2 to 3 cups SHELLED RAW PEANUTS
2 Tbsp. BUTTER
1 tsp. VANILLA
5 to 6 drops RED FOOD COLORING

Mix corn syrup, sugar and cream together; add peanuts and cook, stirring frequently to prevent sticking. Cook until soft ball stage. Remove from heat and add butter, vanilla, and food coloring. Stir until very creamy and fairly cool. Spoon onto waxed paper.

Apricot Balls

8 ounces DRIED APRICOTS
2/3 cup PECANS
1 cup COCONUT
2 tsp.(+) ORANGE JUICE
POWDERED SUGAR

Grind apricots and pecans together in food processor. Combine remaining ingredients, adding enough juice to slightly moisten the mixture. Roll into balls about the size of a walnut. Roll in powdered sugar.

Edith's Spiced Pecans

"At holiday time, I guess everyone has a recipe from Mom. My mother was the world's worst cook. But at Christmas time, she made these great spiced pecans." Shirley Baumbach, Lazy Palms Ranch, Edinburg

1 EGG WHITE
1 tsp. COLD WATER
1 lb. PECAN HALVES
1/2 cup SUGAR
1/2 tsp. SALT
1/2 tsp. CINNAMON

Beat egg white and water (in large bowl) until foamy, but not stiff. Add pecans and mix till all nuts are coated. Mix sugar, salt and cinnamon. Add to nuts and mix thoroughly. Place on buttered cookie sheet (10 x 15) and bake at 225 degrees for 1 hour, stirring every 15 minutes. Cool, then store in airtight container.

Chocolate Crackers

Kelly McCulloch, Alvarado

SALTINE CRACKERS (approximately 40)
1 cup MARGARINE
1 cup BROWN SUGAR
6 oz. CHOCOLATE CHIPS
6 oz. PECANS, chopped

Line a cookie sheet with foil. Place saltine crackers on cookie sheet. Boil margarine and brown sugar for three minutes. Pour mixture over crackers. Bake at 350 degrees for 5 minutes. Remove from oven and sprinkle chocolate chips onto crackers and spread with spatula. Sprinkle pecans on top. Let cool and refrigerate. Break into pieces and enjoy.

Ranch Fudge

"This is a very easy recipe and has never failed. You will never have fudge that you don't know if you are going to eat it with a spoon or have to use an air hammer to cut it." Shirley Baumbach, Lazy Palms Ranch, Edinburg.

2 sticks BUTTER (do not use margarine)
3 bags (6 oz. ea.) CHOCOLATE CHIPS
2 cups CHOPPED WALNUTS
1/4 tsp. SALT
1 Tbsp. VANILLA
1 can (12 oz.) EVAPORATED MILK
4 1/2 cups WHITE SUGAR

In a large mixing bowl, place butter, chocolate chips, walnuts, salt and vanilla. Set aside. Into large heavy kettle, put evaporated milk and sugar. Bring to a rolling boil, stirring constantly with a spiral whisk. Boil hard for 7 minutes. Pour hot mixture over all ingredients in bowl. Stir until blended and thick. Pour into buttered 9 x 13 cookie sheet. Refrigerate for 2 hours. Cut into 96 squares (8 squares across and 12 down).

Christmas Da Tees

"These have been our favorite cookies for many years. They are the first cookies my kids asked for when I start my baking for Christmas." Carmen Dougherty, Marian

8 Tbsp. BUTTER or MARGARINE
1 cup BROWN SUGAR, packed
1 pkg. (8 oz.) DATES, chopped and pitted
2 cups RICE KRISPIES®, lightly crushed
1 cup PECANS, chopped
1/2 cup FLAKED COCONUT
1/2 cup POWDERED SUGAR

In a cast iron skillet, melt margarine or butter. Add brown sugar and dates. Cook over medium heat until well blended. Remove from heat and add crushed Rice Krispies, pecans and coconut. Mix thoroughly. With hands shape mixture into round balls and roll in powdered sugar.

Yield: 5 dozen

Puppy Chow

"Serve this in a new doggie dish with a bow tied around the middle. Use as a centerpiece and fill bowl as needed. A big hit at every Christmas party." Bonnie Dixon, Alvarado

1 stick MARGARINE
1 1/4 cup PEANUT BUTTER
16 oz. CHOCOLATE CHIPS
1 box (17.9 oz.) KRISPIX® CEREAL
1 cup POWDERED SUGAR
8 to 10 oz. DRY ROASTED PEANUTS

Melt margarine, peanut butter and chocolate chips in microwave or double boiler. Put cereal on two cookie sheets. Pour chocolate mixture over cereal and mix quickly. Cool 25 minutes. Put in large bowl and sift powdered sugar on top. Cover and shake. Add peanuts and shake again.

Thumbprints

1 cup BUTTER or
    MARGARINE
1 cup SUGAR
2 EGG YOLKS
1 tsp. VANILLA

2 cups FLOUR
1/2 tsp. SALT
2 EGG WHITES
2 cups NUTS,
    finely chopped

Cream butter, sugar, egg yolks and vanilla. Mix flour and salt and stir into creamed mixture. Chill dough. Roll dough one teaspoon at a time, into balls. Dip in slightly beaten egg whites and roll in nuts or flaked coconut. Place on baking sheet and press thumb into center of each. Bake at 350 degrees for 8 to 10 minutes. Fill the center of each cooled cookie with tinted powder sugar icing or a small amount of currant jelly.

Angel Food Cookies

Give these cookies as gifts to friends. They are delicious during the holidays with coffee or tea.

1 cup SHORTENING
1/2 cup BROWN SUGAR
1/2 cup GRANULATED SUGAR
1 EGG, beaten
1 tsp. BANANA or LEMON
    EXTRACT
1 cup COCONUT

1/4 tsp. SALT
2 cups FLOUR
1 tsp. BAKING SODA
1 tsp. CREAM OF TARTAR
1/2 cup POWDERED
    SUGAR

Mix shortening and sugars until creamy. Add beaten egg, extract and coconut. Sift dry ingredients and mix into the cream mixture. Roll dough into small balls and flatten. Place water in small bowl and powdered sugar into another bowl. Dip one side of each ball of dough first into water and then into powdered sugar. Place on greased cookie sheet. Bake at 375 degrees for about 15 minutes, or until cookies are light brown.

Yield: About 4 dozen.

Chocolate Snowballs

"Recipes, and especially old recipes, are like old friends. They bring back memories of the food we used to eat. We live in a region of good cooks. We have the Mexican food we all grew up with, and here in Fredericksburg we have the best home cooking by German people. This recipe has been a family favorite for over 40 years. It's not Christmas without it." Vangie Huie, Fredericksburg

3/4 cup MARGARINE
1/2 cup SUGAR
2 tsp. VANILLA
1 EGG
2 cups sifted FLOUR
1/2 tsp. SALT
1 cup PECANS, chopped
1 cup CHOCOLATE CHIPS
POWDERED SUGAR

Blend margarine, sugar and vanilla. Beat in egg. Stir in flour and salt by hand. Fold in nuts and chocolate chips. Shape in balls about tablespoon size. Do not flatten. Place on ungreased cookie sheet and bake at 350 degrees until lightly browned. Watch carefully—**do not overbake!** Roll in powdered sugar. This recipe freezes well.

Popcorn Balls

1 1/2 cup POPCORN, popped
2 cups BROWN SUGAR
2 sticks MARGARINE
1 3/4 cup CORN SYRUP
1 can SWEETENED CONDENSED MILK

Pop popcorn and set aside. Boil brown sugar, margarine and syrup for 3 minutes. Remove from heat and add sweetened condensed milk. Boil 3 more minutes. Pour over popcorn. When cool enough to handle, shape into balls. Wrap with plastic wrap. Tie ends with red or green ribbon.

Chocolate Crispies

"This was a cookie my German grandmother would have ready for me to eat when I got home from school." Vangie Huie, Fredericksburg

2 squares BAKING CHOCOLATE
1 stick MARGARINE
1 cup SUGAR
2 EGGS, beaten
1/2 cup FLOUR
1 tsp. VANILLA
PECANS, chopped

Melt chocolate and margarine in a saucepan. Add sugar, eggs, flour and vanilla. Mix well. Spread in a well greased 11 x 13 cookie pan. Sprinkle chopped pecans on top. Bake in a 300 degree oven for 20 minutes. Don't overbake. Cool and cut into big squares.

Sugarplum Divinity

Gum drops add a colorful touch to this holiday delight.

2 1/2 cup SUGAR
1/2 cup WHITE CORN SYRUP
1/2 cup COLD WATER
2 EGG WHITES, slightly beaten
1 tsp. VANILLA
1/2 cup multi-colored GUM DROP CANDIES,
  cut into slivers.

Combine sugar, syrup and water in saucepan and stir over low heat until sugar dissolves. Cook until candy thermometer registers 260 degrees or until it reaches the very hard ball stage. Remove from heat and cool slightly. Beat egg whites until stiff. Pour hot mixture very slowly over egg whites, beating constantly. Continue beating until mixture becomes very stiff and loses its glossy appearance. Beat a few strokes by hand to improve texture. Add vanilla and drop by large spoonfuls onto waxed paper. Decorate with slivers of gum drops by pressing cut edges to candy.
Yield: about 1 1/2 pounds.

Mexican Wedding Cookies

1 cup softened BUTTER
1 tsp. VANILLA
1/2 cup CONFECTIONERS
  SUGAR

2 cups FLOUR
1/4 tsp. SALT
1 cup PECANS, finely
  chopped

Cream butter, add vanilla. Stir to a light and fluffy texture. Add sugar and cream the mixture. Mix flour and salt and add creamed mixture. Sprinkle with pecans. Blend well. Form into 24 balls and flatten out lightly. Bake at 350 degrees for 25 minutes or until light brown.
Makes 2 dozen cookies.

Cranberry Party Bars

1/2 cup BUTTER or MARGARINE
1 cup SUGAR
3 EGG YOLKS
2 cups sifted all-purpose FLOUR
1/4 tsp. SALT
1/2 tsp. BAKING POWDER
1/4 cup WATER
1 tsp. VANILLA
1 1/3 cups (14-oz. jar) CRANBERRY-ORANGE RELISH
3 EGG WHITES
1/4 tsp. SALT
1 cup NUTS, chopped

Cream butter, adding 1/2 cup of the sugar gradually. Beat in egg yolks one at a time. Sift together flour, salt and baking powder; add to creamed mixture alternately with water. Stir in vanilla. Spread evenly in 9 x 12 ungreased pan. Spread with cranberry-orange relish, drained if necessary. For meringue topping, beat egg whites and salt until stiff. Gradually beat in the remaining 1/2 cup sugar until peaks hold stiff. Fold in nuts. Spread meringue over cranberry-orange relish. Bake at 350 degrees for 20 to 25 minutes. When thoroughly cold, cut into squares.

Yield: 48 bars.

Mexican Sombreros

1 3/4 cups FLOUR
1 tsp. BAKING SODA
1/2 tsp. SALT
1/2 cup SUGAR
1/2 cup BROWN SUGAR, firmly packed
1/2 cup SHORTENING
1/2 cup PEANUT BUTTER
1 EGG
2 Tbsp. MILK
1 tsp. VANILLA
48 MILK CHOCOLATE KISSES

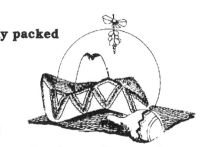

Preheat oven 375 degrees. Combine all ingredients except candy in a large mixing bowl. Mix on lowest speed of mixer until dough firms. Shape dough into balls, using a rounded teaspoonful for each. Roll balls in sugar; place on ungreased cookie sheet and bake at 375 degrees for 10 to 12 minutes. Top cookies immediately with chocolate kisses, pressing firmly until cookie cracks slightly.

Yield: Approximately 4 dozen.

Peanut Brittle

It wouldn't be Christmas without peanut brittle!

1 cup SUGAR
1 cup WHITE CORN SYRUP
1 cup RAW SPANISH PEANUTS
1/4 tsp. SALT
1 Tbsp. BUTTER
1 tsp. BAKING SODA

Put sugar and syrup in a heavy 10-inch skillet. Cook over medium heat, stirring continuously with a wooden spoon. When it is golden (about 10 minutes), add peanuts, salt and butter. Remove from heat and lightly fold in baking soda. Quickly pour into a buttered cookie sheet in three separate "plops." Do not spread the candy as that tends to break the bubbles and will make the candy less brittle. Let cool and break into pieces.

Index

Recipe Contributors

Faye Albertson, Wimberley   32, 34
Arrowhead Mills, Hereford   72-73
Vernie Bailey, Kemp   85
Carol Barclay, Portland   19, 21, 47, 59, 62, 70
Shirley Baumbach, Lazy Palms Ranch, Edinburg   50, 71, 104-105
Florence Belzung, San Antonio   99
Della Brown, Decatur   83
Pam Cole, Holiday   92
Amber Combs, Seven Points   79
Sandra Davis, Holiday   102
Bonnie Dixon, Alvarado   17, 20, 22, 64, 90, 106, 109
Carmen Dougherty, Marion   42, 106-107
El Galindo Mexican Foods, Austin   48
Fran Forbes, Pleasanton   88
Mary Foster, Wellington   23, 33, 60, 70, 77, 103, 107
Jean Fourmentin, Wellington   30
Vivian Gaines, Clarksville   87
Lucille Garcia, Beeville   86
Dorothy Geroianni, San Antonio   79
Guadalupe Smoked Meat Company Restaurant   31
Vangie Huie, Fredericksburg   108-109
Pauline Huneycutt, San Antonio   29
Imperial Sugar Company, Sugar Land 10, 12, 30, 91, 94, 110-111
Jardine's Texas Foods   53
Glenn Koteras, Orchard   41, 42
Debbie Kremling, Sherman   27
Beverly McClatchy, Midland 11, 12, 18, 20, 23, 28,
61, 64, 69, 71, 92, 102-103
Kelly McCulloch, Alvarado   18, 104
Sylvia Meador, Boyd   33
Melba Mullen, Steelville   101
Charlotte Myrick, Wellington   63
Elsie Pierce, Sweetwater   68
Mildred L. Pietzsch, Roscoe   58
Marian Ramsay, Fort Worth   82
Nancy Rhodes, Tenaha   45
Rhonda Richey, Chico   84
Helen Ruetten, Elm Mott   80
San Saba Pecan, Inc.   78
Helen Souther, Chico   60
Talk O'Texas Brands, Inc., San Angelo   22
The Mozzarella Company, Dallas   28, 43-44, 83
Myrtle Thomas, Clarksville   93
Wanda Timmermann, Geronimo   101
Jo Anne Tucker, Chico   98, 103
Lena Vaughan, Wellington   39-40, 89-90
Sally Walker, Coldspring   17
Jody Feldtman Wright, San Antonio   11, 31, 88

More Cook Books by Golden West Publishers

CHRISTMAS IN COLORADO COOK BOOK

Christmas holiday traditions, folklore and favorite foods from the Rockies. Includes recipes from innkeepers, homemakers, and professional chefs. Wide variety of flavors, from *Olde English Plum Pudding* to *Denver Frittatas*.

5 1/2 x8 1/2—120 pages . . . $8.95

CHRISTMAS IN ARIZONA COOK BOOK

'Tis the season . . . celebrate Christmas in sunny Arizona. Read about the fascinating southwestern traditions and foods. Create a southwestern holiday spirit with this wonderful cook book. By Lynn Nusom.

6 x 9—128 pages . . . $8.95

CHRISTMAS IN NEW MEXICO COOK BOOK

Recipes, traditions and folklore for the Holiday Season—or all year long. Try *Three Kings Bread, Posole de Posada, Christmas Pumpkin Pie, Christmas Turkey with White Wine Basting Sauce*, and many more taste tempters! Makes an excellent gift! By Lynn Nusom.

6 x 9—144 pages . . . $8.95

TEXAS COOK BOOK

Over 200 tasty Texas recipes and a side of Texas trivia, too! Chili, barbecue, cowboy, Tex-Mex, stir-fry and many more favorite recipes submitted by Texans to make this book a treat in any state. Learn about Texas traditions and history as you sample the best of Texas!

5 1/2 x 8 1/2 — 144 pages . . . $5.95

BEST BARBECUE RECIPES

A collection of more than 200 taste-tempting recipes. • Marinades • Rubs • Mops • Ribs • Wild Game • Fish and Seafood • Pit barbecue and more! By Al & Mildred Fischer.

5 1/2 x 8 1/2 — 144 pages . . . $5.95

SALSA LOVERS COOK BOOK

More than 180 taste-tempting recipes for salsas that will make every meal a special event! Salsas for salads, appetizers, main dishes, and desserts! Put some salsa in your life! By Susan K. Bollin.

5 1/2 x 8 1/2—128 pages . . . $5.95

CHIP & DIP LOVERS COOK BOOK

More than 150 recipes for fun and festive dips. Make southwestern dips, dips with fruits and vegetables, meats, poultry and seafood. Salsa dips and dips for desserts. Includes recipes for making homemade chips. By Susan K. Bollin.

5 1/2 x 8 1/2—112 pages . . . $5.95

QUICK-N-EASY MEXICAN RECIPES

More than 175 favorite Mexican recipes you can prepare in less than thirty minutes. Traditional items such as tacos, tostadas and enchiladas. Also features easy recipes for salads, soups, breads, desserts and drinks. By Susan K. Bollin.

5 1/2 x 8 1/2—128 pages . . . $5.95

THE TEQUILA COOK BOOK

Taste the spirit and flavor of the southwest! More than 150 recipes featuring tequila as an ingredient. Wonderful appetizers, soups, salads, main dishes, breads, desserts, and, of course, drinks. Includes fascinating tequila trivia. Truly a unique cook book and a great gift item! By Lynn Nusom.

5 1/2 x 8 1/2—128 pages . . . $7.95

CHILI-LOVERS' COOK BOOK

Chili cookoff prize-winning recipes and regional favorites! The best of chili cookery, from mild to fiery, with and without beans. Plus a variety of taste-tempting foods made with chile peppers. 180,000 copies in print! By Al and Mildred Fischer.

5 1/2 x 8 1/2—128 pages . . . $5.95

ORDER BLANK

GOLDEN WEST PUBLISHERS

☼ 4113 N. Longview Ave. • Phoenix, AZ 85014

602-265-4392 • **1-800-658-5830** • FAX 602-279-6901

Qty	Title	Price	Amount
	Arizona Cook Book	5.95	
	Best Barbecue Recipes	5.95	
	Chili-Lovers' Cook Book	5.95	
	Chip and Dip Lovers Cook Book	5.95	
	Christmas in Arizona Cook Book	8.95	
	Christmas in Colorado Cook Book	8.95	
	Christmas in New Mexico Cook Book	8.95	
	Christmas in Texas Cook Book	8.95	
	Christmas in Washington Cook Book	8.95	
	Citrus Lovers Cook Book	6.95	
	Colorado Favorites Cook Book	5.95	
	Cowboy Cartoon Cook Book	5.95	
	New Mexico Cook Book	5.95	
	Pecan-Lovers' Cook Book	6.95	
	Quick-n-Easy Mexican Recipes	5.95	
	Recipes for a Healthy Lifestyle	6.95	
	Salsa Lovers Cook Book	5.95	
	Tequila Cook Book	7.95	
	Texas Cook Book	5.95	
	Wholly Frijoles! The Whole Bean Cook Book	6.95	
	Add $2.00 to total order for shipping & handling		**$2.00**

☐ My Check or Money Order Enclosed. . . . . $

☐ MasterCard ☐ VISA

(Payable in U.S. funds)

Acct. No.   Exp. Date

Signature

Name   Telephone

Address

City/State/Zip

Call or write for FREE catalog

8/95   MasterCard and VISA Orders Accepted ($20 Minimum)

Xmas Tex

This order blank may be photo-copied.